CREATIVE RAW COOKING

MERCÉ PASSOLA AND
EDGARD VILADEVALL

TRANSLATED BY
JULIE GANZ

Skyhorse Publishing

Skyhorse Publishing books may be purchased in bulk at special discounts for sales, promotion, corporate gifts, fund-raising, or educational purposes. Special editions can also be created to specifications. For details, contact the Special Sales Department, Skyhorse Publishing, 307 West 36th Street, 11th Floor, New York, NY 10018 or info@skyhorsepublishing.com.

Skyhorse® and Skyhorse Publishing® are registered trademarks of Skyhorse Publishing, Inc.®, a Delaware corporation.

Visit our website at www.skyhorsepublishing.com.

10 9 8 7 6 5 4 3 2 1

Library of Congress Cataloging-in-Publication Data is available on file.

Cover design by Owen Corrigan
Cover photo credit Becky Lawton

Print ISBN: 978-1-62914-471-9
E-book ISBN: 978-1-62914-914-1

Printed in China

To imagine, create, and produce in the world of the creative raw kitchen is a unique experience in which a person gives the best of his or herself. There exists a constant motivation to discover new textures, tastes, colors, and presentations. The excitement is so big that you are compelled to share it. *A book?* you think. *That is an excellent way to share this excitement!* you conclude. You don't know how to start, but the excitement pushes you and suddenly everything you need emerges, as if you were already prepared.

Thank you, Adriana Ortemberg; you materialized like a fairy godmother, you spun the thread and everything appeared. But then you begin, and you realize you need help . . . and it arrives. Thank you, Javier Medvedovsky; your presence was important. Thank you, Maria Tránsito López; when one doesn't know how to continue, it is good to have you nearby.

We also thank the team at Océano Ambar, and to Jaume Rosselló and Esther Sanz in particular, for the trust they had in our project and their ability to share with us the pleasure of tasting some dishes. We are also grateful for the work of all those who have participated in this book: photographers, typesetters, printers . . . All of them have made it possible for this book to see the light.

Thanks also to Carles Viladevall who, with his presence and support, didn't let the excitement fade.

Of course, thanks to all the people who on this long journey have stayed by our side silently, but always supporting this project.

This book has been a learning experience for us, and an unforgettable experience at that. But it will not be complete until we satisfy a final wish: that the reader gets excited and shares this experience, enjoys and slowly savors the recipes, and lets his or her imagination fly in order to create new recipes.

Thank you for helping us make this dream a reality.

Mercé and Edgard

Contents

Prologue

Nourishing yourself is an act of giving life. It can be achieved out of necessity or out of eagerness, out of routine or out of creativity, with disregard or with feeling. *Creative Raw Cooking* is a book that teaches us to eat with excitement, with imagination, and with passion; it is a book through which we learn to love food and to receive the nutrients with gratitude and satisfaction.

Eating raw foods is the best way to incorporate the sun's energy, which we need, into our bodies in the most organized way possible. But it is also the most conventional and enjoyable way of providing nutrients to our minds and spirits.

The pages that follow are a gift for the senses. Entering the kitchen, and even without turning on the stove, working with our hands through the different textures of the foods, rejoicing after seeing the remarkable colors on the plate, and feeling, upon tasting, the sound and aroma that each ingredient frees, enriches the sensations of our palate and makes the food feel like a true pleasure.

Food also has a positive influence on our emotional state. The enteric nervous system, known as the "second brain" or "abdominal cerebrum," found in our small intestine, consists of a network of very important neurons, such as those of the spinal cord, which frees neurotransmitters like serotonin. This is why what we eat and how we eat it is so important.

Authors Mercé and Edgard show us the result of their explorations in the kitchen after many years of practicing, and they make their dishes come to life with the original idea of naming each one of them for principles about which we can ponder and by which we can live.

After reading it I can say with total sincerity that "I am happy" to be able to present to you this book.

Pedro Ródenas (Naturopathic Doctor)

Introduction

This book is a gift: writing it, sharing it with you, and offering you a small part of the immense possibilities that exist from making new things are all part of the gift.

It pleases us to share the wonders of the world and to encourage people to enjoy those wonders. We like to enjoy our food and to make sure it is the healthiest for the body. We wish for people to be a temple of health and vitality and for them to obtain their maximum potential.

Creative raw cooking is based on raw ingredients and uses techniques that maintain and maximize the original properties of those ingredients. It is a form of eating ingredients full of life and nutrients that also have exquisite flavors, smells, and textures in order to satisfy ourselves and our five senses, especially the palate.

It is a kitchen in which health, gastronomy, and innovation are combined in harmony. A form of nourishing oneself that takes care of us on the inside (thanks to the benefits that the raw foods produce) and the outside (health is also reflected on the skin, in the hair, in the eyes . . .). Thus, it is no surprise that Olympic athletes, movie stars, and singers make the most of all these advantages.

In the field of health, raw foods help us in many situations. To start, they boost the digestive process and improve how well we utilize the nutrients that we consume, which affects our energy, vitality, and well-being. They also help us control our weight, as well as delay signs of aging. And they contribute to preventing and weakening degenerative diseases, as distressing as they are.

In addition, creative raw cooking allows us to discover that it is possible to manipulate raw ingredients with simple techniques that conserve and maximize their potential nutritious value. And not only that, but they also make it possible to experience new recipes that open to us a world of creative possibilities capable of providing our senses with new experiences.

In effect, creative raw cooking is "innovation," since it makes this union of gastronomy and health truly delicious, with surprising results. It is an innovation that, by nature, also causes us to ask ourselves about how we live our life. It is clear, like all the innovations themselves . . .

Our dream is for each person to eat and live as he or she feels that he or she should, since no one knows better than his or herself what is in his or her own best interest. In this book we show a culinary method to doing so, which has produced important benefits. Raw foods, combined with a good physical exercise regimen, appropriate rest, and a positive attitude toward life, have given us feelings of well-being that we hadn't experienced before. Thus, you will find, together with the names of the dishes, references to evoke delightful feelings. Nutrition can start in the mouth, but everything that surrounds us nourishes us if it makes us grow and contributes to our well-being. The words do too. Enjoy this book!

About Creative Raw Cooking

Although the term "raw" may seem like cooking doesn't play a big role,
it will surprise you to discover how much we can do with these foods.

When we decide to eat a raw food, we can consume it in its simplest form; for example, taking a fruit directly from the tree. If this fruit has been cultivated in an ecological form, obeying the natural cycles and their environment, and it has been collected at its optimal point of ripening, we obtain food that supplies its best aroma and flavor and with all its nutritious properties. The feeling that is experienced upon eating a food in these conditions allows us to truly savor our food.

But, in addition to eating it as such, we can transform this same food into a creative form using simple, formal techniques like cutting, squeezing, maceration, and dehydration. Thanks to those techniques, we will give it a different appearance, a different texture, and a different flavor, at the same time conserving a steep nutritional flavor. In this way, we can create endless possibilities in our kitchen and introduce an immense variety of alternatives in our diet.

Using other techniques like the sprouting of seeds and fermentation, not only do we take advantage of the great nutritional richness of the foods, but also we strengthen their properties. With sprouting, above everything in the first days, the amount of chlorophyll, enzymes, and proteins increases. In addition, it is the stage of its development in which the plant reaches its maximum vital force, for it is the ideal moment for engineering it as a food. In fermentation, a great synthesis of nutrients, like vitamins, and large amounts of lactic bacterias that help us to reestablish intestinal flora, are produced.

The cooking that we present in this book is based in principal on these foods: fruits, vegetables, nuts, seeds and grains, seaweed, mushrooms, aromatic herbs, and spices. The use of the techniques mentioned and of these ingredients in our dishes permits us to distinguish the purity, the aroma, and the color of each one of them, at the same time that we enjoy the whole combination.

Raw foods have nourished humanity since its beginnings. The arguments in favor of them are convincing and are supported by a large number of people, including those in the areas of nutrition and medicine, where they support their fine qualities and their direct impact on our health.

These foods produce carbohydrates, proteins, and fats. The carbohydrates are easily absorbed and supply us with energy. The vegetable proteins are not denatured by extra heat and are absorbed by our bodies. And the majority of the fats are not oxidized and are therefore much healthier. These fats have an abundance of vitamins, minerals, fiber, phytonutrients, and, above all, enzymes. The enzymes play an important role in the digestive process through their role as catalysts that speed up biochemical reactions.

Digestion

This process consists of breaking down the foods that are consumed into their simplest parts until they've become elements that can be utilized by an organism's cells.

The nutrients that are present in food are composed of molecules, which are more or less complex, that have transformed themselves so that the cells of our body can obtain the energy that they need for their growth. The digestive enzymes are in charge of beginning the decomposition of the molecules of the nutrients until achieving sufficient simple elements so they can be used to form useful new molecules for the regeneration of the organism. Therefore, good nutrition relies on the quality of your digestive process, as well as that of the foods that are consumed.

Digestion starts in the mouth

The digestive process starts in the mouth with the act of chewing and mixing saliva with the foods. During the chewing they are ground up and shredded until they have a suitable texture and consistency to circulate through the esophagus and to easily arrive at the stomach. Saliva starts this process by aiding in the breakdown of starches with the help of an enzyme called amylase.

Next, the digestive process continues in the stomach. Here the enzyme pepsin, together with great amounts of gastric juices and hydrochloric acid, is in charge of breaking down the proteins. Proteins are made up of amino acids that further prepare the remaining food for the rest of its journey down the digestive tract.

Once the food leaves the stomach, it passes through the small intestine, where it soon comes in contact with juices from the pancreas. Various digestive enzymes work to complete the job of decomposition not accomplished by the pepsin of the stomach. Another enzyme, the amylase, ends what the saliva started and finalizes the decomposition of the starches, and another, lipase, is in charge of, together with bile, decomposing the fats in fatty acids.

The bile that separates the liver and that is stored in what is called the "gall bladder" assimilates, in this phase, according to the needs that are required by the type of food that is consumed. Its function is central in dividing the fats, to the maximum, with the objective of facilitating the action of the enzymes present in the pancreatic juice.

As the assimilated food is now treated, it continues its journey through the intestine, where broken-down elements of the nutrients are absorbed into the body through the intestinal wall. From there they travel through the bloodstream and are distributed to all the cells of the body. The cells are then in charge of their own feeding process, and, therefore, for the regeneration of the tissues that the cells are a part of.

The rest of the material that's not absorbed continues its journey until it arrives at the last section of the intestine, called the large intestine. Here, the greatest amount of the water is absorbed, as well as some minerals and also organic acids produced by what is called the "intestinal flora" present on the walls of the intestine. Finally the cast-away residue arrives at the final stage of its journey in order to be ejected.

The function of the intestinal flora

In the large intestine, there are a large number of bacteria present, called "intestinal flora," which benefit the health of the body. Amongst their functions, they participate in the defense of the organism, preventing eventual infections produced by contaminated foods with damaging bacterium that surpasses the barrier of hydrochloric acid present in the stomach. Furthermore, they help synthesize the vitamins. Therefore, it is very important to protect the intestinal flora in order to avoid disruption. One way of reinforcing it consists of eating fermented foods, like rejuvelac or sauerkraut, which we will speak more about later on. These types of products, as we will see, enrich the intestinal flora in an extraordinary way.

Enzymes

● Digestive enzymes. Participate directly in the process of digestion in the way we have mentioned before. There are numerous digestive enzymes and, for the most part, they synthesize themselves throughout the digestive system. When the enzymes can't participate or they can't produce enough, the digestive process is not fully completed, the nutrition begins to weaken, and it retains food that is partially digested that starts the processes of fermentation and decomposition. These processes constitute an additional problem by producing toxic residue that passes to the blood and leads to consequent damage and wearing down of the organism.

● The enzymes that are found in raw foods. They are very important since each food includes conditions for their own digestive process. But it should be advised that they don't resist heat and they are destroyed starting at 102.2 degrees Fahrenheit. This is the motivation behind avoiding cooking the foods that are included in recipes in this book. Some of their functions include: facilitating digestion, helping to take advantage of the nutrients, avoiding the production of toxins, saving enzymes of the organism, and reducing the energy expensed by the organism. All of that benefits one's health and beauty in the broadest use of the word.

● The metabolic enzymes produced by different organs of the body. They participate, like their name indicates, in the processes of metabolism, particularly the following: elimination of waste, the promotion of a healthy immune system, and the regeneration of the tissues.

But if they are found at temperatures higher than 102.2 degrees Fahrenheit (39 degrees Celsius), they begin to be destroyed and their contributions can't be taken advantage of. Hence the importance of consuming them raw.

Other significant components of food digestion include: fiber, which stimulates intestinal peristalsis and, by consequence, prevents constipation; and water, which is the best way to fulfill your daily liquid requirement. They also provide us many sustentative benefits with antioxidant effects that help us delay aging.

Additionally, the depurative power of raw foods must be emphasized. They clean out toxins and stored residue that interfere with the good function of the cells and the organs from the organism. The first sign of their effects is that the physical appearance improves, for they help you take care of your beauty; your skin becomes smoother and firmer, your lines of expression soften, and your eyes acquire the clarity and the brilliance they had when you were younger.

Raw foods also help to prevent or alleviate health problems, since they heighten resistance. Also, combined with well-balanced physical exercise, they help to control and maintain the natural weight of each person.

They also contribute by providing the greatest physical and mental energy, fundamental in order for us to be more alert and awake, to think with more clarity, and to have more excitement for experiencing new things. Therefore, it is no surprise that in the little time that it takes to integrate raw foods into our diet, we feel more agile, happier, in a better mood, stronger, and more able to concentrate.

The recipes in this book are prepared with the majority of people and palates in mind and with the idea that to eat is a party. Everyone can adapt them using the different techniques mentioned, not only based on their tastes, but also in the proportion of the raw foods that is agreeable. If it's preferable for you to eat without salt and/or with more aromatic herbs, try it! If you prefer to have fewer dried fruits in a dish, try it! If you prefer sweeter recipes, try it! The dishes that we propose to you are only a point of departure so that you try and create your own dishes.

The words "to cook" seem to be tied inevitably to heat. As a result, we tend to think that raw ingredients are only mere companions. With the help of this book, raw foods previously left as garnishes, now become the heroes of the plate. They turn into foods that affect our health and allow us to enjoy the food for the flavors, aromas, and textures that are a part of them, as well as for the novelty and imagination that they awaken in us.

Creative raw cooking is not only a food for the body, but also for the soul. It awards us with moments of well-being and awakens in us authentic passion for life.

Basic Ingredients

When we selected the ingredients that we used to prepare the recipes, we intended for them to be ecologically grown, that they were raised naturally, that they are in season, and that they have been harvested at their optimal point of maturation. In this way, the results are more delicious and nutritious.

When using raw ingredients in their natural state, keep in mind that they can differ in their water content, their degrees of sweetness, their texture, etc. In effect, there are parameters that can vary a lot from one food to another depending on the farmer, where they're farmed, the climate, and the species.

Raw products, since they are live material, change with the passage of time. In order to familiarize yourself with them, it is easier to recognize which are the best and in what moment it is most suitable to use them in the kitchen, since they vary in the amount of flavor and how they affect the final result of the recipe.

Fruits

Fruits are principally carriers of carbohydrates, and complemented by proteins, fats, minerals, vitamins, enzymes, fiber, and water. They act as strong antioxidants of quick and easy assimilation, and they contribute in an important way to equalize, fortify, revitalize, detoxify, and purify the organism.

Fruits are present in a multitude of therapeutic recommendations, as they also form a part of the "juice therapy" programs, treatments based on the virtues of the juices (see recipe **I am air**, p. 212). A multitude of types exist that offer us a great diversity of forms, textures, colors, aromas, tastes, and an ample variety of nutrients, with the possibility of constructing beautiful presentations, pleasant to the senses.

In addition to enjoying them in delicious juices, fruits also can be eaten alone, for breakfast, as a snack, or as a part of any meal. In this way, they are ideal in salads and a multitude of dishes (see recipe **I am excellent**, p. 81), thanks to their delicious flavor and texture. It is recommended, of course, to avoid eating them for dessert, considering that the quickness and ease of their digestion in front of other types of foods would lead to their deterioration upon having to adapt to the rhythm of those other foods. They can also be prepared in a delicious combination of two or three types of fruit, except melon and watermelon, which you should eat solo, to enjoy a better digestion. Diverse studies done by specialists show the direct relationship between the consumption of fruit and the reduction of the risk of cardiovascular diseases as well as the majority of chronic illnesses that appear with age.

They are therefore treated as the true "vessels of health."

Types of fruits

● Drupes. Fruits with a full, thick pulp that encloses a seed in the center. For example cherries, plums, dates, mangos, peaches, etc.

● Pomes. Fruits with a smooth skin and consistent pulp that encloses the central part in which various seeds are lodged. Apples and pears are part of this group.

● Berries. Thick fruits with a good amount of juice, without a central pit and with many seeds. Examples include raspberries, grapes, etc.

● Citruses. A type of modified berry with a thick pulp separated in segments in which the seeds are found. The most well-known ones are the orange, the lemon, the mandarin, and the grapefruit.

● Pepos. Another type of berry with a hard skin, of a large size, and with many interior seeds scattered between their pulp, as in the case of the watermelon, or grouped in the center, as in the case of the melon.

● Infructescences. Fruits that grow despite a grouping of flowers (inflorescences), whose ovaries, upon maturation, are broken in a single fruit. One characteristic example is the tropical pineapple.

Dried Fruits

The drying process is undertaken for their consumption, in good conditions, for a long time after harvest. It is essential to indicate that the denomination "dried fruits" isn't the same as "nuts."

They are fruits that have been subjected to a process of drying (extracting part of the water), whether it is exposing them to the sun's heat or subjecting them to a partial dehydration in appropriate devices.

Amongst the most popular variety are raisins, figs, dates, plums, and apricots (or dried peaches). All of them have a very high nutritional value due to the high concentration of nutrients produced by reducing the amount of water that they had in the fresh state. As a result, they should be consumed in moderation.

They constitute a type of food that is very beneficial for the health because they contain an abundant source of carbohydrates (monosaccharide sugars). These are incorporated with speed into the bloodstream without needing to overload the digestion process, for they supply free energy for the body in no time. Its sweet flavor should be noted, due to the presence of these sugars in a high concentration. This important amount of caloric nutrients is supplied to us at almost 300 kcal for 100 g, which suggests that they should be consumed in moderation and chewed well.

In addition to the sugars (carbohydrates) mentioned, dried fruits contain a concentration of proteins, fiber, minerals, vitamins, and trace minerals. Amongst the most prominent minerals are potassium, phosphorus, calcium, and iron. For the vitamins, the most prominent are the B vitamins, most importantly B1 (thiamine), B2 (riboflavin), B3 (niacin), and B6 (pyridoxine), which combine in the metabolism of the aforementioned sugars and, therefore, help the cells take advantage of their energy.

For all their nutritious richness, their consumption is comfortable, especially when going on excursions or long walks. They are easy to consume and quick to digest, and their energetic contribution is high. Another value comes in its use as a natural sweetener, serving as a sugar substitute with incomparable advantage (which contributes to their many nutritious components) compared to the common white sugar (see recipe *I am light*, p. 178). They also serve as flavor enhancers in some recipes because of the concentration of the flavor that is produced, for example, in the strawberry, the orange, or the pineapple (see recipe *I am a pleasure*, p. 184).

Soaking dried fruit in water will substantially improve the digestibility.

In whichever case, it is best to chew them very well.

How are they dried?

The method for drying fruit has evolved for a long time throughout history. At the beginning, the procedure consisted of exposing the fruit directly to the sun in an airy environment that permitted the elimination of the evaporating water. This natural process has been imitated by various apparatuses, each time becoming more perfected, that they achieve the same effect. In order to obtain this effect, you need to subject the fruit to a current of warm air inside a controlled enclosure so the humidity is discharged to the outside. No matter which procedure you use, some dried fruits acquire a color that is darker. This change, which is merely aesthetic, has been considered not as good (by some of the public) from a commercial point of view. Therefore, to correct this circumstance, in some cases an additive is added (sodium sulfite) that embellishes its appearance. Without a doubt, this substance can cause allergies in some people, a motive for consuming dried fruits without adding additives.

Greens and Produce

Each season offers us its particular assortment of produce and greens. It is then when they are found in their best moment and at the best price, so we can choose them according to our tastes and appetites in order to prepare delicious and nutritious recipes.

They are herbaceous plants with edible parts, whether they are their leaves, their roots, their flowers, or their fruits. Some are valued for more than one of their parts. For example, in the case of beets, the roots, leaves, and core of the vegetable can be used as well as the fruit and the flowers.

In general, greens can be eaten mashed in soups and juices (see recipe *I am valiant*, p. 75), just like they are cut up in salads (see recipe *I am a decision*, p. 86). Their great variety of flavors and colors provide a freshness and a spring of healthy resources to our daily dishes (see recipe *I am a game*, p. 118).

All of them have a great amount of water and various proportions of minerals, carbohydrates, proteins, fats, vitamins, enzymes, and other essential substances for the organism, in addition to fiber. Fiber is important because it contributes to the intestinal traffic and helps us avoid constipation. In addition, the fiber exercises a protective function from degenerative illnesses. This group, it can be said, serves as a complete storage facility.

Amongst the minerals, the function of magnesium should be noted for its presence in the chlorophyll molecule (mainly in the green leaves). Magnesium participates in the formation of the bones, in muscular relaxation, and in many other vital functions. The greens and vegetables are key carriers of antioxidants of great potency, as in bacteria (provitamin A) and vitamin C. The former contributes to the good state of the skin and mucus, and the latter helps the body's defensive system, amongst many other functions. Other vitamins that contribute in an important way are those from group B, with key results for the good function of the nervous system.

Greens or produce?

Greens, as their name indicates, are characterized by their green color, which comes from chlorophyll. As a general rule, leaves, stems, and some flowers (such as the artichoke) are considered greens, and thus the tomato is considered "produce" and not a green.

Weight-loss diets

Greens and produce, engineered in a form that is raw and natural, don't make people fat, even when they are consumed in large portions. For this reason they are included, preferably, in the majority of weight-loss diets.

Grains and Legumes

One characteristic of grains and legume seeds is that they are "concentrated" foods that can't be consumed until they are harvested. We can always use them in the creative raw kitchen once they are sprouted.

With the technique of sprouting (see the part named "Techniques: sprouts"), not only is the loss of its natural properties avoided, but also its nutritious value is strengthened, since this is the best way of taking advantage of these traits.

Through sprouting, the seeds give up being grains and are converted to sprouts. It is this stage in which the sprouts have all their strength, the enzymes, vitamins, minerals, chlorophyll, proteins, and simple sugars. It is the moment in which the plant is found with the most vital energy, which is the ideal moment to be consumed. We can incorporate sprouts in a great variety of dishes (see recipe *I am confidence*, p. 143 and *I am expansion*, p. 137), although, due to its nutritious richness, it is not necessary to consume them in great quantities.

Sprouting is a very easy technique to carry out. In order to begin this process, you'll need to know about the best seeds, which we enumerate here:

- **Lentils, chickpeas, adzuki beans, mung beans, and soybeans.** All of them provide protein and are a good source of iron and phosphorus.
- **Quinoa seeds.** Although it is considered a pseudo-grain because it's not from the family of traditional grains, it contains a high amount of starch in its natural form, which is converted to sugars upon sprouting. It also provides calcium, iron, and phosphorus.
- **Wheat.** The sprouts of this grain are rich in proteins, calcium, iron, and vitamin B.

In addition to grains and legumes, in the creative raw kitchen we can also grow other types of seeds: sunflower, pumpkin, mustard, Chinese cabbage, buckwheat, radish, etc.

Nuts and Seeds

Within the group of nuts and seeds we find almonds, hazelnuts, walnuts, sesame seeds, sunflower seeds, pumpkin seeds, etc. They are characterized as such because the edible part, which is the seed, contains a very small amount of water.

These foods are very concentrated in nutrients and represent a good source of energy for those of any age, always taken in moderation. They are especially rich in:

- **Fats,** with predominance in the good fats: mono-unsaturated fatty acids, like oleic acid, and polyunsaturated fatty acids like linoleic acid (Omega 6) and linolenic acid (Omega 3). These last two are essential for the formation and the maintenance of the membranes of all types of cells of the organism, above all the nerve cells.
- **Proteins and minerals.** Amongst these, and most prominently, magnesium, potassium, calcium, phosphorus, iron, and zinc are found.
- **Regarding vitamins**, B1 (thiamine), B3 (niacin), folates, and vitamin E all stand out.
- **Their high content of fiber** favors intestinal movement, rather than constipation.
- **Varieties of and numerous bioactive substances** beneficial for the organism, amongst which the following stand out—phenolic compounds (as strong antioxidants) and phytosterols.

All of these kinds of nuts and seeds benefit the general nervous system. Thus they are recommended both for improving performance at work, as and for exercise, as they help produce an intense level of activity, especially for those that are subjected to stress. Due to their high energy level, they are recommended for people who are physically active. In the kitchen we can use them in many dishes; the creativity can bring us to spectacular results (see recipe *I am all heart*, p. 196).

Because of their elevated proportion of fats, they are difficult foods to digest, and thus they should be chewed very well and consumed in very moderate portions. It is recommended to soak them for some hours before ingesting them so that the seed starts its vital activity, the enzymes multiply, the inhibitors are freed, and the flavor is improved while they become more assimilable. Also, we can grind them with water or with rejuvelac until they acquire the consistency of cream or liquid, lighter still for our body (see recipe *I am perfection*, p. 209). If we use rejuvelac, the resulting food can be considered predigested and releases great amounts of organic nutrients.

Seaweed and Other Algae: The Greens of the Sea

Presently there is knowledge of 24,000 distinct species of seaweed and other forms of algae and, just like with land plants, only few varieties are used in human nutrition. The algae also have roots, stems, and leaves, but with a much simpler structure.

There are those of an extreme simplicity, as is the case of those that are composed of a sole cell, but other kinds exist that create true natural walls on the ocean floor.

Regarding their nutritional contribution, we can determine that this type of green also has chlorophyll, which combines in the formation of hemoglobin and in the purification of the blood. Regarding its vitamin composition, its richness in vitamin E, provitamin A (beta-carotene), and group B vitamins stand out. Thus, it is very important that seaweed and other forms of algae are included in foods (see recipe **I am truth**, p. 115).

Sea vegetables contain large quantities of mineral salts and trace minerals. Principally, they are rich in iodine, a mineral that regulates the function of the thyroid gland and is responsible for burning off the ingested sugars. They also contain good doses of magnesium, potassium, calcium, and phosphorus. The amount that fits on a soup spoon is enough to supply the organism all the essential minerals for an appropriate cellular metabolism. This class of plants also contains essential fatty acids in addition to containing an important provision of vegetable proteins, incomparably extraordinary for their contribution of all the essential amino acids in an appropriate proportion and, in addition, is easy to digest.

For all of that, sea vegetables possess many virtues: they are depurative, remineralizing, weight-reducing in their effective way of filling you up, and they produce mucilage, a type of fiber that activates and benefits the intestinal functions, avoiding constipation.

Different types of sea greens

Seaweed and other algae are classified in eleven groups, but those that are used for nutrition can be simplified into three:

Brown seaweed
They grow primarily in cold waters, forming great extensions of submarine meadows. One example is the laminaria seaweed (*Phaeophyceae*), a genus that exists primarily in the North Atlantic Ocean and North Pacific.

Some of the best known types of brown seaweed are:

Seaweeds contain a basic, important element particular to them: alginic acid. This acid collaborates in the elimination of the heavy metals of our organism, such as lead, mercury, arsenic, etc., which we could have absorbed through respiration (in the air) or through our diet (in foods).

- **Kombu.** Contains abundant potassium and calcium. It is used to give flavor to the dishes.
- **Wakame.** In particular calcium, potassium, vitamin C, and vitamins from group B stand out.
- **Hijiki.** It has a great amount of potassium, iron, and calcium.
- **Arame.** Of mild, subtle flavor, it contains, principally, iodone and calcium.
- **Other edible sea vegetables** are rich in alginic acid, magnesium, calcium, iron, and sulfur.

Red seaweed

This one is the group with the most species, as it contains about 4,000 on the whole planet. The most used, in human nutrition, is the variety known as "dulse," which contains a large proportion of proteins and minerals (iron, potassium, and phosphorus). It also includes the nori algae, rich in proteins and provitamin A (beta-carotene).

Blue algae or blue-green seaweed

Although it is a group of algae that we don't use habitually in the recipes of creative raw cooking, we mention them for being a group that is quite common in alkaline algae from tropical or subtropical zones with high salt content. Thousands of species exist, but the best known are, without a doubt, spirulina and chlorella. Traditionally they have been used in vegetable juices. Blue seaweed is a good source of protein, iron, and group B vitamins.

Mushrooms

In addition to being very versatile foods that give us an extensive range of flavors, textures, and aromas once prepared, some mushrooms also possess interesting therapeutic properties that are worth knowing about and enjoying.

Mushrooms have been consumed for ages in their wild state. Many edible varieties exist so that the experience and popular flavor has been identified and incorporated with the group of freely available foods. They have a very short life span and they decompose rapidly so that after a long time, they have optimized farming techniques that permit their preparation all year round.

Mushrooms emerge and leave the surface when they are given appropriate environmental conditions of humidity and temperature. They reproduce by means of "spores" that fall and are scattered on the surrounding ground, providing a place of origin for the new mushrooms.

In the past, mushrooms were classified as part of the vegetable kingdom, but because they don't have chlorophyll and are therefore unable to carry out photosynthesis, in the second half of the last century, a new group called "fungi" was specifically formed for them.

In their composition we can emphasize the water, the element that is present in greatest proportion, its contribution of group B vitamins, and minerals like phosphorus, potassium, and iron.

Mushrooms provide us an extensive range of flavors, textures, and aromas that we can enjoy once prepared. Their forms are very diverse and, combined with various mushroom cutting techniques, offer us an ample array of attractive possibilities of presentation for different dishes (see recipe I am an abundance, p. 111).

And all of that with a value added, which is that some of them have therapeutic properties. Above all are the mushrooms of Eastern origin, used in distant times in traditional Chinese medicine. The curative qualities of some of them have been conveyed. Such is the case of the shitake mushroom (*Lentinus edodes*), which in addition to its fine and exquisite flavor, contains a potent action to the defenses of the organism and help reduce cholesterol, amongst other properties. It can be found both dry and fresh. Another Eastern kind that is beneficial is the enoki mushroom (*Flammulina velutipes*), a true stimulus of the immune system, which has a soft texture and a weak flavor. In other parts of the world, farmed mushrooms, with a fine stalk and a small cap, which are presented in bundles, are consumed. For its part, the local, best-known kinds of mushrooms, like the pine mushroom and the champignon, are valued for the antibiotic substances that they contain.

Buying and conservation

It is preferable to consume very fresh mushrooms. Therefore, it is advisable to choose the pieces that are most firm and, above all, free of blemishes. On the other hand, those that present a dry base, a broken cap, or are discolored, sticky, or creased should be rejected . . . as all of those are unequivocal signs of their lack of freshness. It is advisable to keep in mind that mushrooms are perishable and they only last a few hours at room temperature. We can prolong their freshness by keeping them in the refrigerator up to three or four days. Beforehand, it is true that they should be washed well. But even better is to scrape them superficially with a knife or use a cloth over them, to avoid moistening them, so they don't get water-logged and lose their good qualities.

Aromatic Herbs, Spices, and Flowers

These three ingredients provide a characteristic taste and aroma, and hence are used to season, modify, or highlight the flavor of the foods. To know them and use them well allows you to create dishes that are appetizing, interesting, and varied. Of course, who doesn't like a dish that is well-seasoned and presented? In these first perceptions of the dish, you find the beginning of a favorable digestive process.

Aromatic herbs

Those known as "aromatic herbs" are not indispensable in our habitual diet, since their nutritious contribution is reduced to a small amount of mineral salts, fiber, and beneficial substances. They are always used in very limited quantities, adjusted to the taste of each person with just the right amount to stimulate the senses (mainly taste and smell), which is pleasantly perceptible. In order to achieve this, they tend to undergo a process of being ground into small pieces, at the end of which they liberate their organoleptic properties, or those that affect the senses (see recipe *I am expression*, p. 154). You should avoid overusing aromatic herbs on your foods, since if they are used in excess they can result in a seasoning that's too strong or even disagreeable.

In addition to the flavor that the dishes provide, aromatic herbs stand out for their interesting medicinal properties. The antiseptic and antifungal effects of some of them, like the thyme and sage, are only a small example. The greater part of them have a stimulant effect on the appetite and digestion, and favor the digestive secretions. Many of their varieties also possess carminative ability, which contributes to reducing the production of the intestinal gases.

Spices

Principally, spices are obtained from the barks, rhizomes, or seeds of certain aromatic, normally dry, plants. They are appreciated for their flavors, aromas, and colors that they contribute to the dishes (see recipe *I am hope*, p. 152). Although each one contributes to good health in a concrete manner, in general they are characterized as aids to the digestive process, helping to direct and better assimilate the nutrients, and also to reduce the formation of intestinal gases. They also have certain antimicrobial actions and they tone the body. Some spices also have the ability to stimulate circulation.

Again, as in the case of aromatic herbs, spices should be used in moderation, in small doses adjusted to personal taste, since use in excess can cause unpleasant setbacks. That being said, people who need to continue low-salt diets can benefit from the moderate use of these condiments.

Flowers

In addition to their beauty and exquisite aroma, flowers offer us new textures and delicious flavors that can be taken advantage of in order to enhance your recipes. Habitually they are sold after having been grown industrially in order to ensure their freshness in addition to their innocuousness, since they are not all edible. We should also make sure that they are not treated chemically. If you have a good knowledge of the edible species, they can be used from the wild, since harvested with the proper respect to their surroundings, they give us very authentic flavors. That being so, we should be vigilant of not harvesting them in contaminated zones like, for example, the side of a highway, as the gases that the cars emit can carry toxic elements. In some cases, we can use flowers as simple decoration and in others to provide a special touch to our dishes. Using flowers in our recipes contributes to the elegance, freshness, and color while at the same time becoming a party for the senses (see recipe **I am illumination**, p. 218).

Other Ingredients

Honey, the agave plant, and the stevia plant are suitable sweeteners to enrich our dishes with appropriate flavors. Upon continuing we will discover many things about them and about other very interesting foods.

Honey

For its great content of carbohydrates (mainly fructose and glucose, in addition to a small amount of sucrose), it is a food that puts a great amount of energy at the organism's disposal almost immediately. It also contains small amounts of vitamins from group B (B1, B2, and B6). Amongst the minerals that it produces, it emphasizes potassium, magnesium, iron, calcium, and phosphorus. It also contains enzymes like invertase, important as much for facilitating digestion of this food, as it is for helping the digestive process of other carbohydrates that can be found in foods. In addition, it is in charge of transforming the sucrose into simple molecules, like fructose and glucose. Other components are amino acids, flavoids, organic acids, etc., which are still being investigated for their biologic activity.

Apart from its use as a sweetener and helping the digestive process, its invigorating and expectorate effects stand out as well.

Agave

The syrup of the agave, obtained from a plant by the same name, "blue agave" (*Tequila Weber*), is a transparent molasses that resembles clear honey, with a sweet taste. It is used as a sweetener with a low glycemic index, which contributes to reducing the level of lipids (fats) in the blood, the risk of heart conditions, and the effect of hypoglycemia.

At the same time, it is a sweetener that is well tolerated by those who suffer from diabetes, since it helps to regulate the levels of insulin. We should also emphasize its high content of fructooligosaccharides, which, in addition to facilitating the intestinal function, contributes to enhancing the defenses of the organism due to its beneficial actions on the balance of the bacterial flora.

Stevia

This small bush of very sweet leaves, bright green in color, originates from Brazil and Paraguay. Traditionally it has been used as a sweetener as much for foods as for drinks, with beneficial effects. Today it is used in the preparation of marmalades, drinks, and sweets in general, thanks to its sweetening capacity that doesn't add too many calories. Amongst its therapeutic properties, the following stand out: its ability to regulate the concentration of glucose in the blood (anti-diabetic) and its diuretic, antibacterial, and vasodilator effects.

Salt

Called "table salt," its basic composition is sodium chloride. It is used to provide flavor to foods, to give texture to foods, and also for its preservative abilities.

It can be obtained through a process of evaporation of ocean water and in this case its composition is much richer than simple sodium chorlide. Other sources that provide salt include the subterranean mines in which deposits of distinct varieties have formed.

We can find salt in several varieties, including from the Himlayas, as well as salt from Great Britain and Maldon salt. And according to the industrial process to which they have been submitted, we can choose between the specialized salts, herb salts, smoked salts, etc. In all of them different flavors, textures, and colors can be distinguished which permits us to season our plates with special touches. Thus, it is important to recognize not only its flavor but also the size of its grain and the ease of dissolving each type.

Finally, despite the subtle flavors that you can obtain with this product, it is very important to emphasize that salt should be used with much moderation and to take advantage of the alternatives that we have at our disposal: aromatic herbs and spices.

Oil

In the market we find many varieties of oil: olive oil, sunflower oil, almond oil, flax oil, walnut oil, hemp oil, pistachio oil, pumpkin seed oil, etc. All of them, of course, have been extracted from their corresponding seeds and fruits. The dissolved liquid results in a fatty material. Some are saturated fats (not usually recommended for health reasons) and others are unsaturated (much healthier). If we use any, we should use only the unsaturated kind. In the recipes that we have collected in this book we have used, mainly, first cold pressed olive oil that is organically farmed. Without a doubt, others can be used, with flavors that are very unique to offer those special touches, such as the pumpkin seed oil, the flax oil, or the walnut oil. Despite the ample varieties we have at our disposal and the benefits they produce, oil is a food that we should not abuse since it adds many calories to our diet in the form of fat.

Tamari

It highlights the flavor of the foods, although it should be added in a very small quantity because of its elevated level of sodium. It stands out for its richness in amino acids and in antioxidant substances. In the market, we can find two types of tamari:

- **Soy Tamari** is subjected to a process of fermentation with water and salt.
- **Tamari Shoyu,** is also obtained via fermentation but with wheat base in addition to soy, water, and salt.

Both products undergo a period of various months of fermentation.

Miso

Originating in Asia, it has a strong salty flavor. It is a product based on fermented soy, which, optionally, can present variations if in the preparation process you add another food like rice or barley in addition to sea salt. In its production, a simple technique is used that consists of putting the soy or the chosen mixture in a container, putting pressure on it, and letting it ferment for many months, or sometimes years, depending on the variety. The miso provides carbohydrates, minerals like iron, magnesium, and calcium, essential amino acids, and a little fat. Its main quality is that it purifies, thanks to its yeast, enzymes, and live microorganisms that free the intestines from the residue of the process of assimilating the nutrients. It also helps in cases of flatulence, constipation, and diarrhea. It is used to provide flavor, above all, in soups, sauces, cheeses, etc. It's best to aim for unpasteurized.

Olives

It is an ingredient of great tradition that the Egyptians, Greeks, and Romans used in their dishes. Within the great variety of kinds and sizes that still exist today, we mainly find two colors: green ones and black ones. The green olives are smaller and of a fruity, light flavor, while the black ones are more intense. Those that we find in the market have been subjected to various processes in order to eliminate its bitterness and often they are prepared with aromatic herbs, garlic, salt, etc. We can also get dried olives already salted or sun-dried (these have a more noticeable flavor). They usually are black in color when the fruit is mature.

The olive adds personality and pleasure, providing character and a different touch to the dishes. The main component of the olives is the water and its energy contribution is between moderate and high. They contain a lot of grease, predominantly from fatty, unsaturated acids and, thus, the healthier kind. They also provide other substances of dietary and nutritional interest: fiber, vitamins, minerals, and antioxidant substances.

Capers

The caper is the floral bud of a blackberry bush. It has been consumed since ancient times as an ingredient in many of the traditional dishes from the Mediterranean region. It is shaped like the olive but of a smaller size.

Its flavor is a little bitter and it goes well with a variety of foods as it offers a characteristic touch to the whole dish. Thus, it can be used in an ample variety of dishes and recipes. Its composition presents an elevated proportion of water, carbohydrates, and very little fat.

Cocoa beans

The cocoa bean has been declared one of the most universal gastronomic pleasures. It is used in the kitchen to prepare an endless number of delicious recipes that satisfy many palates: ice cream, pastries, crackers, sauces, soups . . . And also, it is used to make chocolate.

It is a very energetic food, with a high concentration of carbohydrates and fats. Calcium, magnesium, potassium, phosphorus, iron, and copper are amongst the minerals found in cocoa beans. With regard to vitamins, they provide those from group B (B1—thiamine, B2—riboflavin, and B9—folic acid), as well as vitamin E (antioxidant). The cocoa also contains theobromine, a substance that is attributed to a strengthening action and stimulant for the nervous system. Theobromine is a substance that acts like caffeine from coffee or theine from tea but with stimulating effects that are less intense, and it is responsible for the bitter taste of the cocoa. Other key components of the cocoa are the flavonoids, which carry out a very strong antioxidant function.

Carob beans

This is the name given to the seed of the carob, a tree from the Mediterranean that comes from the family of leguminous plants with a fruit in the shape of long green beans of a brown color, like chocolate, when they are matured. These are used as a substitute for cocoa beans.

It differentiates itself from the cocoa bean in that it's naturally sweet, lacks stimulant substances, and hardly contains fat. Its vitamin value also is notable, as it contributes important quantities of vitamins from group B (B1—thiamine, B2—riboflavin, and B3—niacine) and provitamin A (beta-carotene). It has proteins and minerals including calcium, magnesium, phosphorus, iron, and silicon. Its great potassium and low sodium content also stand out.

There are many condiments or ingredients that we can add to our recipes. Here we have described some of them, but there are many more: vinegar, umeboshi plums, wasabi, date sugar, etc. Challenge yourself to include them in your dishes and extend your culinary horizons. Many of these more obscure ingredients can be found at health food stores and food co-ops or online. Always choose ingredients that best conserve their natural properties and offer healthy benefits.

Equipment

Preparing the recipes from this book in a kitchen that is well organized and equipped is a true pleasure. The utensils help us manipulate the foods and to work in an enjoyable, simple manner.

In our case, in addition to the usual utensils of a regular kitchen, the use of certain equipment offers us a large range of cuts and textures that allows us to prepare splendid dishes, sauces, soups, shakes . . . while saving work and time. It is much better to acquire those of high quality that comply with our expectations and needs, without overloading the closets with junk that you don't use afterwards.

Moving forward, we detail the instruments that are most useful:

Kitchen robot

It is a very helpful tool in this kind of kitchen. Thanks to its diversity of accessories, it is ideal to grate and roll different thicknesses, to grind and mix ingredients, both dry and moist, as well as knead to make breads, biscuits, pizzas, and a great variety of different dishes.

Blender

The blender has to be strong in order to grind the fiber of the foods that, in this way, will be easier to digest. A blender is ideal to make soups, shakes, drinks, sauces, milks, yogurts, seed cheeses, etc.

Juicer

Useful to make fruit juices and vegetable shakes. In addition to a good juice, the juicer helps us enrich our sauces, shakes, drinks, etc., with finer, more delicate textures, and also to prepare liquid ingredients to use them in marinades.

Dehydrator

Its job is to dehydrate many types of foods and is a basic tool in making crackers, biscuits, breads, pizzas, hamburgers . . . Amongst the systems of domestic dehydration that can be found, the most suitable is that which has a system of horizontal dehydration, with a motor in the back. In this way it assures a dehydration of the foods that's more homogenous. It is also useful that the trays can be retracted in whatever moment in order to increase the interior volume and to introduce foods of greater thicknesses and/or heights. If it also has a thermostat, it will permit you to regulate the temperature to 102.2 degrees Fahrenheit at a constant level, and to conserve the food's enzymes. A dehydrator is a good tool to dry out excess fruits and vegetables and to keep them at your disposal for many recipes.

Other Utensils

With the objective of getting the most out of the raw foods, it is necessary to get utensils that are practical and of good quality. To have them in full view makes things easier.

Grater-mandolin

It is very useful and it saves a lot of time at the time of grating and presentation of the fruits and vegetables. It permits us to slice in an easy, quick way.

Spiral grater

It is a machine that, as its name indicates, allows us to obtain spirals and noodles from vegetables and fruits. It is also ideal for making special dishes and decorations.

Vegetable peeler

A tool that is very simple and available in any cooking supplies store. It is very useful—and not only for peeling vegetables, but also for rolling and for making very fine cuts.

Coffee grinder

It can serve to grind and to obtain flour from small seeds such as linseeds and sunflower seeds.

Wheatgrass Juicer

It is a juicer specifically for preparing this type of juice, since the conventional juicers don't have the proper mechanism. The juice is extracted by pressing the herb and not crushing it. It can be manual or electric.

It is also important to have some good knives for peeling and cutting. We find ceramic knives very interesting because the vegetables don't rust upon cutting them. At the same time, it helps to have a good cutting board, an accurate balance, and some measuring cups for liquid ingredients.

Of course, some tools and materials make our work simpler and more enjoyable. Such is the case of the citrus squeezer, a garlic grater, a mortar, a potato masher, tools for creating sushi and nigiri, colanders, and different-sized mixing bowls.

Make your kitchen an enjoyable place!

Culinary Techniques

To eat food just as nature has created them has its enchantment and pleasantness. But, in our culture, we are accustomed to manipulating the foods and preparing different dishes with them, and to show our happiness, converting it into a party. In fact, it is a way of enjoying our great creativity, while also nourishing ourselves.

The techniques that we explain here are respectful to the ingredients and allow us not only to conserve their nutrients, but also to increase them in some cases. In this way we obtain a food of superior quality that is much more nutritious.

These techniques also allow us to alter the shape, taste, texture, aroma, and color of the foods so that we can create new, delicious, and varied dishes.

Blending

Blending the foods permits us to incorporate liquids into our diet in the form of juices, shakes, milks, cocktails, sauces, and soups that collaborate on the fundamental mission of keeping the body well hydrated.

In order to prepare them, it is only necessary to blend the ingredients that we want, with whichever machine that allows us to do so. As a result, liquids are obtained with delicious natural flavors, which, also, are a source of very effective enzymes, vitamins, minerals, and antioxidants, so that the digestion is very fast, and, consequently, nutrients pass rapidly through the blood. Although they are treated as liquids it is important to realize that it is necessary to insalivate them correctly.

In order for us to best enjoy these dishes it is important that we prepare them ourselves and that we use ecological products. Those that exist in the store are generally pasteurized, and thus they have lost part of their freshness and enzymes. To delight our dinner guests with recipes recently made is a true pleasure, in addition to being a form of putting to practice our creativity and taking care of ourselves.

The blended foods can have different consistencies, from very liquidy (like a juice) to heavier (like a shake, cream, or sauce), and between them an endless amount of textures applied to different dishes. When we use fruits and vegetables, in addition to enjoying authentic juices (see recipe **I am aroma**, p. 204), we can enjoy authentic shakes, soups, and crèmes. In order to prepare them it is ideal to have a strong beater (i.e. Vitamix) to grind the fiber. In this way, the digestive process itself is quicker and assimilates better (see recipe **I am exceptional**, p. 213).

On the other hand, we can also liquefy seeds and grains. If, once sprouted (see process of sprouting), we grind them with water, we will obtain many different kinds of milk: almond milk, quinoa milk, hazelnut milk, and pine nut milk (see recipe **I am**

Wheatgrass juice can be liquefied with a special machine for this purpose. It is an apparatus that separates the juice from the part of the fiber that is not assimilable through the organism. The drink that results is excellent for their beneficial properties.

a feather, p. 208). Other ingredients like sweeteners, fruits, vegetables, and more can be added to these milks, and in doing so, we can make wonderful creations that can be served as a base for sauces and soups, and in this way, can obtain magnificent recipes that, with them, can be served as a base for sauces and soups (see recipe **I am excellent**, p. 81). We can also liquefy them with rejuvelac to prepare yogurts and creams (see recipe **I am clarity**, p. 160). To use the seeds and grains in this way provides benefits to our health, since it is a very light way of introducing into our dishes some naturally concentrated foods.

Sauces are also made through the liquification of various ingredients, wholly or partially. Sauces have a very important purpose in the creative raw kitchen, due to the fact that a good sauce can transform the plate in a radical way and can provide the necessary balance and at the same time offer a satisfying taste (see recipe **I give thanks**, p. 155).

Cutting

In our kitchen, the process of preparing the dishes is as important a factor as their presentation. For this reason, it is very important that the foods are cut and prepared in a certain way.

For example, regularity in thickness allows them to absorb the condiments in a uniform way. It is an art that is perfected with practice but that can be supported by small utensils of which it is possible to find a countless number in the market and which help us achieve the appropriate precision. Upon presenting the foods with regular cuts we obtain the feeling of order and tidiness, although in some dishes it is interesting that there's a sense of anarchy in their forms. A particular style of cutting is the "signature" of the dish.

Some of the cuts most frequently used in the kitchen have defined names and measurements, such as:

Slices

This is cutting across in the form of discs, with more or less thickness, foods that are spherical or cylindrical like tomatoes and cucumbers. There exist utensils of the mandolin kind that are able to achieve fine, uniform slices. With an instrument that presents an undulating blade, you can make slices (of a zucchini or cucumber, for example) with a wavy border. In this case, in addition, we can obtain mesh slices with small holes upon spinning the food a quarter of a turn in each round. Another kind is the cut in oval slices, by only bending the piece that is used a few degrees for the cut. For example, this is done with carrots, turnips, parsnips, bananas, etc.

Mirepoix

This is the cut of the ingredients in a form that is irregular or more or less cubed or whatever the piece in question permits. It generally signifies "carved up" without mattering that they lack a defined artistic shape.

Segments

This cut is achieved by dividing a rounded food into four or eight parts or more. It is used primarily for onions, tomatoes, apples, etc. In the case of oranges and other fruits like it, segments are its natural form and it is advised to keep it that way.

Punctured

It is called "punctured" since it's cut in very small pieces. Foods with very prominent aromas and tastes like onions, ginger, and basil are usually cut this way The normal process is to cut it into pieces and to repeat the process until obtaining the desired texture.

Strips or Sticks

Cutting in sticks or strips consists of cutting the food in rectangular shapes of approximately 2/5 inches (1 cm) thick and a variable length according to the piece that is being used. It can also be made with other thicknesses according to the kind of preparation or

the aesthetic of the dish it's being used for. Thus, cut ingredients offer a great diversity of possibilities.

Julienne Cut

Derives from the French *julienne*. It describes a cut in very fine strips of whichever kind of food, principally produce and greens. In the case of pieces of a good volume, first they are cut in fine pieces (of one or two millimeters, or 1/25–1/12 inches) and afterwards the small, thin strips are made. In this last operation, and in trying to save time, the pieces are prepared in a pile, one on top of the other, and in this way, with each cut, so many tiny strips are made at once from the pile.

Jardiniere

This cut consists of cutting ingredients such as carrots, parsnips, beets, etc., into small pieces or strips about 1⅕ inches (3 cm) in length by approximately ⅕ inches (half-cm) wide.

Paysanne

It is a cut derived from the jardinière of a similar thickness, but of smaller length, from ⅖–⅘ inches(1–2 cm) in length.

Chiffonade

A cut that's very useful when it comes to leafy vegetables, like lettuce, chard, spinach . . . It is a cut in which you make elongated, very fine pieces. Thus a leaf of appropriate form is rolled and clean cuts are made. Once cut, the leaves look as if they are fine hairs.

Diced

As its name indicates, foods are cut in small cubes (with sides of equal size). It is easy to do this if the strips were previously cut, or, even easier, with the help of a certain kind of tool. According to its size, different steps are taken.

Brunoise

It is called this because it's a cut in the form of a very small cube of less than 1/10 inches (3 mm). Some appropriate utensils exist for this type of cut, which we got into previously and, in one blow, the small, diced pieces are made.

Balls

Consists of getting small, rounded pieces that can be of different diameters based on the utensil employed. It is achieved with the help of a tool in the form of a small spoon applied to the ingredients with a firm core such as zucchini, apples, papaya, melons, etc.

Spiral

It is achieved with firm foods, like carrots, beets, or even zucchini, which are passed through a machine that spins the ingredient against a knife, which can be of different sizes. The result is spirals or rolled strips of different dimensions, and also noodles of different caliber (from big thickness to angel hair). This cut can be used for decorations or to get vegetable spaghetti.

Macerating

When we talk about macerating, we refer to putting a food in contact with other ingredients for a set time (minutes, hours, or even days), with the end result being that it absorbs their properties and is transformed.

It is a process that we can achieve in a liquid medium, where the food is submerged during preparation, or in a dryer environment, in which the food is put in contact with other ingredients, creating a modification in its texture, color, flavor, and/or aroma.

This process is used to alter any kind of food, be it a fruit, vegetable, mushroom, or seaweed and amongst the ingredients that we can use to macerate, we have listed many different options:

- **Lemon or lime juice.** It prevents the foods from oxidizing after cutting and it helps to conserve its original color, instead of the dark color from oxidation. It is especially useful in the case of produce like artichokes and carrots or fruits like avocados, apples, pears, and bananas. It provides acidity to the preparation and also serves to dispel bitter and spicy flavors (see recipe *I am tenderness*, p. 105).

- **Salt.** It helps to extract the water from the ingredients. A very clear example is with zucchini, that upon cutting it into rolls or pieces and adding salt, it loses the water and acquires a bland, totally malleable texture. It happens with the majority of fruits and produce, but in different ways. Salt also provides that salty flavor to the dish, but if only a little bit is used, it serves, simply, to highlight the flavors (see recipe *I am intelligence*, p. 120).

- **Spices and aromatic herbs.** They provide some very characteristic flavors and aromas. They are used to highlight, vary, or complement the taste of the meal. Some also have a light effect on the texture of the food that is macerated. They usually accompany liquid preparations such as lemon juice, tamari, olive oil, agave . . . (see recipe *I am present*, p. 134).

- **Tamari.** It strengthens the taste and provides intense flavor and saltiness. Goes well with mushrooms (see recipe *I am splendor*, p. 132).

- **Olive oil.** When greasy material, such as olive oil, is added to the dish, it softens, it absorbs its characteristic flavor and aroma, and it acquires a very smooth texture. It makes for a good partner to aromatic herbs, spices, and salt. It is also very useful in avoiding rapid oxidation of ingredients such as artichokes or carrots (see recipe *I am elegance*, p. 110).

- **Liquid preparations (juices, milks, sauces).** The macerated ingredient absorbs the liquid preparation and its characteristics.

- **Water.** Necessary to rehydrate dried foods and ideal to attenuate flavors in general. Together with salt it serves to reduce the bitter taste of foods like eggplant (see recipe *I am spectacular*, p. 106). It provides flexibility to the texture.

● **Agave.** The sweet taste of the agave is absorbed by the macerated ingredients. Upon absorption of part of the liquid solution, the food acquires a smoother texture (see recipe *I am celestial*, p. 189).

The temperature plays an important role in macerating, since when the environment is hotter, the changes take place much quicker. It is interesting to experiment with macerating in the sun (see recipe *I am illumination*, p. 218). Knowing the effects of the environmental temperature on the ingredients allows us to get more refined textures and tastes.

Macerating also is used to conserve foods. For example, to add salt or olive oil to certain ingredients conserves them for much longer.

Sprouting

Sprouting is nothing more than facilitating the conditions so that the life that is sleeping in whichever seed wakes up. So that this process is achieved, the seed needs to find the appropriate environment and depends on the necessary water, oxygen, and heat.

Sprouted seeds are one of the most nutritious foods that we know. They are eaten as such, with salads, or as an ingredient of various dishes (see recipe *I am a game*, p. 118). Simple to grow, fresh, tender, authentically flavored, and fine, they are a compendium of virtues and as a result are easy to digest.

The Romans, Greeks, Hebrews, as well as the Egyptians used them, not only for their nutritional properties, but also for therapeutic purposes. In actuality they have been rediscovered upon confirming their magnificent contributions.

A source of life

Few foods provide so much nutrition and vitality like sprouted foods do. When they germinate, the seeds increase their nutritious capacity, they are full of energy and at the time they easily assimilate through the organism.

Upon finding favorable conditions for their growth and development, the "inhibitors" (substances in charge of maintaining the survival of the seed) are dissolved, and it is when the manifestation of the life is initiated. The enzymes are multiplied to generate the metabolic reactions of growth and it is the moment in which the sprouts start to appear. The seeds are converted to plants and their nutritional content increases to the maximum with amino acids, vitamins, minerals, chlorophyll, and enzymes. It is the moment in which the vital energy of the seed is in its critical point, when its complex nutrients are transformed into simpler forms and are, therefore, easier to digest. Therefore, it is at that point when it is ideal to consume them, since all that stored energy is transferred to our body.

What occurs when a seed germinates?

When the seed finds the appropriate conditions in its environment and it has the necessary heat and humidity, it increases in volume through the absorption of the water. The enzymes are activated and start to transform their complex structures into others that are simpler and easier to digest and assimilate:

- The inhibitors decompose and are eliminated.
- The starch turns into simple sugars (maltose and dextrin).
- The proteins are converted to amino acids.
- The fats are converted to fatty acids.
- The mineral salts multiply.
- The synthesis of vitamins increases.
- Chlorophyll synthesizes.

Types of sprouted seeds

Today, it is easy to find sprouts in food stores, but we can also get them from the home, in a simple, economic way. With a small quantity of seeds, their volume increases between two and ten times, depending on the type used; after a short time, fresh, thin sprouts appear. Here we emphasize two types of sprouts, those of hydroponic farming and the greens, which are grown in the ground.

Sprouts from hydroponic farming or in glass jars

They receive this name because they only grow in water. You don't need dirt or fertilizer to grow them, since we can grow them in our own kitchen.

What material do we need?

- Organically grown seeds.
- Glass jar, preferably one with a wide opening.
- A flexible mosquito net.
- Rubber band to attach the mosquito net to the jar's opening.

How do we sprout the seeds?

1 Add a spoonful of seeds to a glass jar and add water (to double the volume of the seeds). Let it soak for 6–7 hours (the majority need this range of time, but you can consult the timetable in this chapter according to the seeds used). It is important to use good-quality water, without chlorine.

2 Once soaked, place the mosquito net covering the opening of the jar and attach it with the rubber band. Drip dry the seeds and wash them two or three times or whatever is necessary so the water stays clean. Once drained, incline the jar 45 degrees, top down, careful not to pile them in the same place but rather distributed along the length of the container. Let it rest, for example, above a strainer, in a warm place where light won't directly hit it. A cloth can be used to cover them so that ultimately the seeds get less light, but it is important to let the air enter.

3 Every day the seeds are rinsed to maintain the humidity. Depending on how hot it is, they will have to rinse off for more or less time. In general, if it is winter, a single time is usually sufficient, while in the summer it should be done a couple of times. Almost all germinate in a period that fluctuates between one and seven days, depending on the kind of seeds.

There exist many other methods for sprouting seeds from hydroponic farming in which different materials are used such as bags, baskets, drainers, or apparatuses built specifically for sprouting.

Sprouted greens

The growth of these sprouts is achieved with soil. A little more time and space is needed for this than for hydroponic farming, but we get very fresh products that are of the best quality, full of energy and chlorophyll. This way of farming produces beauty in the house, as if it were an interior garden of small green sprouts. They can also be cultivated outside, only with the appropriate temperature; the ideal temperature is between 64.4 and 71.6 degrees Fahrenheit (18 and 22 degrees Celsius)

What material do we need?

- Organic seeds with nuts.
- Two rubber bands of two centimeters (8/10 inch) in size, at the most.
- Naturally fertilized soil.
- Garden sprayer to allow for very fine irrigation.

How do you grow germinated greens in the house?

1 Put a spoonful of seeds with nuts to soak in water in the glass jar and let it rest for 6–7 hours (the same advice as for the hydroponic farming).

2 Once past this time, they should be washed, drained, and left inside the jar (proceeding the same way as for hydroponic farming), inclining it 45 degrees, top down, until they germinate. Wash them one or two times a day, depending on the temperature, until the sprouts are half the length of the seed, and it is then when we can plant them in the soil.

3 Prepare a tray with soil, and scatter the sprouts on top, but without placing them on top of each other. Water them with a garden sprayer, only so it's moist, and cover it with another tray to protect it from the light and maintain the moistness.

4 They are placed for two or three days in a warm place and protected from the sun and the air currents. It is advisable to water them with a garden sprayer to maintain the moistness, but with much caution because the seeds are very fragile and any brusqueness can interfere with their growth.

5 Days later, take off the top tray, water it once a day in the winter and twice in the summer, or whatever is necessary to maintain the moistness until the sprouts can be harvested, that is usually between seven and ten days, until they can be revealed.

6 To collect the sprouts, they are cut at soil level with a sharp knife or with scissors.

The excess soil can be recycled to make compost.

Wheatgrass: source of nutrition

After discussing the sprouted greens, it is important to pause at the topic of wheatgrass because in the case of wheatgrass, the blades (fine leaves), which are very hard, are not ingested. Rather, a juice is made with them. Manual machines or special electric machines are used for this process (see chapter dedicated to kitchen equipment), and thus regular blenders don't work well in this case.

Wheatgrass juice is full of nutritious and beneficial properties for your health. It has all of the essential amino acids, is very rich in vitamins, minerals, and trace elements, and it also possesses a great amount of enzymes and chlorophyll. It is a very energetic, easily assimilable, and rejuvenating drink for the organism. Amongst the benefits that it offers, it contributes to the elimination of toxins, the regeneration of the digestive system, and also regenerates the skin and hair and stimulates the production of hemoglobin (see recipe *I am extraordinary*, p. 216).

Germinations of hydroponic farming

Name of the seed	Time to soak the seeds	Time to germinate in the jar
OIL SEEDS		
Sunflower	6–8 hours	1 day
Pumpkin	6–8 hours	1 day
Sesame	6–8 hours	1 day
Almond	24–48 hours	Can be used after soaking
Hazelnut	24 hours	Can be used after soaking
Walnut	6–8 hours	Can be used after soaking
Pine nut	2–6 hours	Can be used after soaking
Cashew	2–6 hours	Can be used after soaking
Macadamia nut	2–6 hours	Can be used after soaking
Linseed	minimum 1 hour	Can be used after soaking
GRAINS		
Soft wheat	8–10 hours	1–2 days or until the sprout is the length of the seed
Rye	8–10 hours	1–2 days or until the sprout is the length of the seed
Oats	8–10 hours	1–2 days or until the sprout is the length of the seed
Buckwheat	30 minutes	1–2 days or until the sprout is the length of the seed
Millet	8–10 hours	1–2 days or until the sprout is the length of the seed
Quinoa	8–10 hours	1–2 days or until the sprout is the length of the seed
Khorasan wheat	8–10 hours	1–2 days or until the sprout is the length of the seed
Spelt	8–10 hours	1–2 days or until the sprout is the length of the seed
Rice	24 hours	3–7 days or until the sprout is the length of the seed

Chickpeas	8–12 hours	2–4 days or until the sprout is ½ the length of the seed
Lentils	8–12 hours	2–4 days or until the sprout is ½ the length of the seed
Mung beans	8–12 hours	2–4 days or until the sprout is ½ the length of the seed
Azuki beans	8–12 hours	2–4 days or until the sprout is ½ the length of the seed
Peas	6–8 hours	Can be used after soaking
OTHERS		
Alfalfa	6–8 hours	4–6 days
Radish	6–8 hours	4–6 days
Cabbage	6–8 hours	4–6 days
Clover	6–8 hours	4–6 days
Fenugreek	8–10 hours	4–6 days
Mustard	6–8 hours	4–6 days
Broccoli	6–8 hours	4–6 days

Germinations from the soil

Name of the seed	Time to soak the seeds	Time to germinate in the jar	Time to germinate in the ground
Sunflower with shell	6–12 hours	1–3 days or until the sprout is the length of ½ the seed	7–10 days
Soft wheat	8–10 hours	1–3 days or until the sprout is the length of ½ the seed	7–10 days
Buckwheat	12 hours	1–3 days or until the sprout is the length of ½ the seed	7–10 days

Fermentation

Fermentation of foods has been practiced in many cultures and for a long time.
Today we also use it to make some older recipes and to create new
ones with all the culinary and nutritious advantages.

Lactic fermentation, the most common kind in our kitchen, provides carbohydrates from the seeds (sesame, sunflower, almond . . .) or vegetables (cabbage, beets, turnips . . .). During this process, bacteria are created that help to maintain or reestablish intestinal flora responsible for a good assimilation of nutrients.

Fermented foods are full of enzymes and are considered predigested because they serve to transform the complex structures of the nutrients into simpler components. The starch is transformed into maltose, and then that's transformed into glucose, which eventually becomes lactic acid. The proteins, for their part, are partially digested and converted to amino acids and the chains of fatty acids are modified until they become simple fatty acids.

The environmental temperature is a factor that plays an important role at the time of fermentation so that as soon as the temperature is warmer, fermentation is achieved faster.

In our kitchen we produce various fermented foods, including:

Rejuvelac

This is the name of a drink that is made through fermentation of water with the germinated seeds of wheat. It is one of the most nutritious drinks and tonics that exists as it incorporates all the nutrients of the wheat in a very assimilable way with a great amount of enzymes, strong presence of vitamins B, C, and E, proteins, carbohydrates, and large quantities of beneficial flora (lactobateria and lactic acid). (See recipe *I am regenerative*, p. 214).

It can be ingested either as a drink or as part of other recipes. In cases where we drink it on its own, there is no limit in quantity, although it is better to start small (for example, 30 ml, or .13 cups). It can also dissolve in water and get a softer effect. To the extent that our body is accustomed, we can increase the quantity. Its antioxidant capacity and its content of beneficial microorganisms for digestion makes it a very appropriate drink in cases where you've had a food that is heavier than you are used to.

It can form part of other recipes such as soups, sauces, other drinks, cheeses, yogurts, and seed creams (see recipe *I am energy*, p. 70).

Seed cheeses

Rejuvelac is used as a ferment to make delicious cheeses based on oleaginous seeds (almonds, sunflower seeds, pumpkin seeds, cashews, pine nuts . . .). These provide us with a large quantity of enzymes and lactobacteria in addition to fats and easily absorbed proteins (predigested).

To obtain them, soak the seeds (as if you were germinating them), and once the soaking time has passed, drain them. Place them in the blender vessel with the rejuvelac (about a two fingers-width) and grind them. Once this is done, let the mixture drain in a cotton cloth at room temperature for four or five hours minimum. If we want a cheese with better consistency, we can reduce the amount of rejuvelac and, thus it will not need draining. We will put it directly in a glass jar, covering it with a cotton cloth, so it ferments. Although the length of time of fermentation may vary, realize that the longer it sits, the stronger is the flavor of the cheese. The pleasure of the intensity of the aroma of the rejuvelac can also vary, which depends a lot on how it has been prepared. Once the appropriate time passes, it can be consumed; this is the moment of adding other ingredients, such as onion, broccoli, spices, aromatic herbs, etc. Finally, keep it in the refrigerator for a few days (see recipes **I am a dancer**, p. 162 and **I am patience**, p. 161).

Creams and seed yogurts

With the same beneficial properties that the seed cheese has, you can make creams and yogurts.

In the case of the creams, the seeds should be soaked (as if you were germinating them) and, once the soaking time has passed, drain them and grind them with rejuvelac until obtaining the desired texture (see recipe **I am laughter**, p. 160).

Depending on the texture and the seed that is used, you should adjust the amount of rejuvelac used. Other ingredients can also be added to get different flavors. It can be used as a base or as an ingredient for sauces, soups, drinks, dishes . . .

In order to make yogurt, follow the same instructions as the cream, but use a greater quantity of rejuvelac (see recipe **I am clarity**, p. 160). It also permits various culinary alternatives whether you're using it as one ingredient in a dish or as the base of different dishes.

Sauerkraut

It is a fermented food with a large tradition in Europe. Although cabbage sauerkraut is the best known, sauerkraut can be prepared with a variety of ingredients: beets, carrots, turnips . . . It can be consumed on its own, together with other ingredients, to prepare sauces, soups, drinks, or accompanied by other dishes. The liquid resulting from the fermentation can be drunk as an appetizer or served as salad dressing.

If you're trying it for the first time, its flavor does not leave you indifferent: it is bitter but with all the sugars present from the produce. Its chemical composition is what makes its taste so characteristic. Full of lactic bacteria, it is a food with many nutritious properties that facilitate digestion, purify the blood, contribute enzymes to the organism, and boost the appetite. It also stimulates the dissemination of the beneficial intestinal flora and it provides a lot of vitamin C.

It is a form of eating "root" produce that is predigested, thanks to fermentation and the enzymes (see recipe **I am stimulating**, p. 147).

Dehydration

To dehydrate a food in our kitchen you must reduce its water content, still respecting to the maximum its nutritious qualities. It is a process that helps us above all in two ways: on the one hand, it is perfect to modify flavors, textures, forms, aromas, and colors in the ingredients and the dishes and, on the other hand, allows us to keep the nutrients.

This process can be achieved with the sun, in an oven, or with a dehydrator (see chapter on "Equipment").

The subtle flavors and nutritional structures of the foods can be modified to a great extent on account of the temperature but they are conserved when the foods haven't been exposed to more than 102.2 degrees Fahrenheit (39 degrees Celsius). Therefore, when we put the foods in contact with sources of heat under this temperature, the foods may change, but their vital enzymes and nutrients are conserved. The dehydration allows us to conserve the principal properties of the distinct ingredients, in addition to benefitting us in many other ways.

In the old days, they used the process of dehydration to dry out and store foods and to conserve them for long periods of time, and in doing so to prepare them when they were needed. Today we also use dehydration to conserve ingredients like produce, fruits, aromatic herbs, seeds, and mushrooms.

During the process of dehydration, the foods change their form, texture, flavor, aroma, and color. Their size becomes smaller due to the loss of water, the texture changes depending on the type of food, and it can become more coarse, dryer, and harder, but it also can be softer, crisper, and more malleable. The flavor and the aroma become more concentrated, and the colors become more intense. To utilize all these possibilities allows us to create never-ending varieties. Here we will show you some:

Fruits

Upon dehydrating fruits, as they lose water their texture softens at the same time that their original flavor becomes more intense. We can detain the process the moment that it seems appropriate to incorporate the fruits into our dishes. With an apple, for example, we can imitate a state of being partially cooked, which has delicious results (see recipe *I am imagination*, p. 192).

With the most advanced process and with less water, the fruits, once they are dried, have, on their own, a very delicious flavor and are ideal for satisfying whatever palate, above all those of kids. Dried apples, pineapples, pears, mangoes, or figs have heavily concentrated nutrients, and, in this state, sweeten at the same time that they thicken the texture of a recipe (see recipe *I am success*, p. 185).

Produce and greens

Produce, when dehydrated, also lose water at the same time that they soften and their taste becomes more concentrated. For example, fresh peppers are smooth and hard, but as the water begins disappearing they soften and wrinkle, as if they had been baked (see recipe **I am passion**, p. 124).

Once dehydrated and cut in the shape of a snack and seasoned to our liking, they are converted to chips, a very nutritious option (see recipe **I am multicolored**, p. 146). They can be totally dried onions, carrots, tomatoes, or beets, and with their intense flavor they are ideal to add to sauces, drinks, soups, or whatever dish to which we want to strengthen the flavor (see recipe **I am communication**, p. 153).

Aromatic herbs

As we have seen, aromatic herbs serve to season any kind of culinary preparation. They are usually used fresh, considering that in this form the flavor of the recipes is much smoother and lighter. Obviously, they can also be dried out in order to be able to resort to using them when we don't have fresh ones on hand. For that, either use a dehydrator or simply place them in a place that is dry, fresh, and dark, covered between cotton cloths.

Seeds

Once soaked and sprouted, we can dehydrate the seeds. When they are dry they can be kept for other occasions or in order to make seed flour for our dishes. In this way, we obtain flour with many more nutrients from the sprouting (see recipe **I am outstanding**, p. 194). If before dehydrating the seeds we marinate them with aromatic herbs, spices, or agave, for example, and we dry them out, recipes like delicious almond curry or caramelized walnuts can be created. If we dehydrate a sauce of oleaginous seeds with greens and produce cut in strips, we will surprise ourselves with some magnificent "tempuras" (see recipe **I am cunning**, p. 140), as if they had been passed through fire, but with colors that are livelier and much more enjoyable. A mix of different seeds, ground with herbs and spices, and optionally greens and produce, or fruits, can be converted to excellent croquettes or fritters, or stuffing for stupendous dishes (see recipes **I am an explosion**, p. 144).

Grains or legumes

Once sprouted, they can be included in recipes that need a dehydrator to obtain a particular texture and flavor (see recipe **I am a star**, p. 135).

Mushrooms

Mushrooms that are fresh and marinated reach refined, surprising flavors. But, also, via a quick dehydration process, they can achieve brilliance (see recipe *I am cooperation*, p. 112).

Dried-out mushrooms can be conserved for a long time.

In the same way that foods in the process of dehydration, or those already dehydrated, offer us different culinary possibilities, we can also use ingredients that are totally dehydrated and rehydrate them (according to what we need). We can do this with water, olive oil, seed milk, sauces, or whatever other liquid preparation, to incorporate them into our dishes (see recipe *I am the journey*, p. 72).

With dehydration we can create never-ending variations of foods, for example:

Crackers

From combinations of soaked seeds (sunflower, flax. . .), grains or sprouted legumes (buckwheat, lentils), greens and produce, fruits, and/or seasonings (depending on your taste), we can make crunchy crackers. You just need to extend the dough, with the desired texture, on top of a sheet of teflex (a non-stick sheet), and the sheet over the tray of the dehydrator.

Once you've exceeded the drying time for the top of the cracker, turn it over, now without the teflex sheet, until obtaining the perfect level of desiccation (see recipe *I am compassion*, p. 168).

Breads

Flour from dried fruits and seeds, and/or flour of sprouted grains (almonds, linseed, wheat, etc.) can be used. The ingredients soak (according to the time chart for soaking and sprouting, p. 54), are dehydrated, and after are crushed until obtaining the flour. We can also add other ingredients such as: fruits, greens, spices, or aromatic herbs, giving us endless possibilities to make different types of breads. Once kneaded, they are dehydrated in portions, either sliced or rolled, always making sure that they're not too thick, so that they're easier to dehydrate (see recipe *I am serenity*, p. 166).

Crepes

One of the properties that defines the crepe is its flexibility. Flexibility is achieved by putting in the dehydrator a dough that, when it is dried to a certain level, permits a sufficient plasticity. It can be achieved with ingredients like: agave and flour of dried fruits; fruits like the apple, pear, banana, pineapple, and avocado; or linseed or zucchini. (see recipe *I am a party*, p. 182).

Pizzas

Pizzas enable us to play with distinct flavors of the dough, considering that we can use the flour of different dried fruits or grains with fruits, greens, or aromatic herbs and spices. In terms of toppings, we also have many options, like lightly dehydrated or marinated greens, mushrooms, cheeses, and olives. (see recipe *I am expansion*, p. 137).

Snacks

Biscuits, granolas, dehydrated granola bars of nori seaweed, etc. All of them are a representation of a multitude of possibilities. Amongst them, biscuits, highly regarded by the majority of people, can be prepared in various ways, but those made with dried fruits and fruits usually have much success (see recipe *I am gratitude*, p. 200).

Granola is a good alternative, accompanied by almond milk and partially or completely dehydrated fruits (see recipe *I am fire*, p. 195).

Dehydrated algae granola bars are leaves of nori algae stuffed with whatever kind of paté made with a base of vegetables, dried fruits, and seasonings. They are rolled up and dehydrated.

Pastries

One option is the simple combination of dates and almonds to achieve a pie crust. We dehydrate it and fill it with fruits and marmalades that we like (see recipe *I am a celebration*, p. 190). Oleaginous fruits (almonds, cashews, macadamia nuts. . .), some sprouted grains, dehydrated fruits, and seasonings serve to sweeten dough with numerous possibilities and textures. They can also be accompanied by fresh ingredients, marinades, semi-dehydrated ingredients, etc.

Dehydration also allows for other possibilities, many of which are used in the gourmet kitchen and the imitation kitchen, which tries to present recipes that are usually made with ingredients cooked with fire, using the bases of the creative raw kitchen (see recipe *I am patience*, p. 161). It is a way of achieving a cultural kitchen based on raw foods.

KEEP IN MIND

- **Good quality.** It is important to use good quality foods, that are well cleaned and at their optimal point. The better they are in their natural state, the better they will be dehydrated. It will be noted in the flavor, the aroma, and the color. If for example, fruits that aren't fully matured are used, upon desiccating them the flavor will be accentuated, but they won't reach the point of ultimate sweetness that we hoped for.

- **Shape.** It's not necessary to dehydrate the whole fruits, but rather they can be cut into pieces or cut in layers.

- **Factors that affect the length of time.** The length of time of the dehydration process depends on factors like:

  - **The size and thickness.** The greater the thickness and size of the food to dehydrate, the more time that will be required to dry it out; similarly, the smaller and finer the food, the easier and quicker the process is.

  - **The amount of water that the food being dried contains.** A more liquidy preparation requires more time than one that's more dense.

  - **The environmental temperature.** If the climate is cold it will take longer than if the temperature is warmer.

  - **The environmental humidity.** When the environmental humidity is elevated, we will need more time for desiccation.

  - **The type and quality of the apparatus used.** The more uniform and effective the desiccation, the less time and better quality the dehydration will have.

- **Conservation.** Fresh ingredients, as well as partially dehydrated ingredients have a limited time of conservation. The less water that a food has, the longer the time of conservation. An ingredient or preparation that is well desiccated can be conserved for a long time. In order to save it, it should be kept in a tightly closed jar and placed in a fresh, dry, and dark place. The temperature of the place should be stable, without changes.

The Development of the Flavors

The intensity with which we perceive the flavors depends on various factors: on the sensitivity of each person (that is influenced by their age, state of health, habits . . .), by the concentration of the flavor and the aroma of the foods, by the interaction between the mixtures that we make, by the amount of water in the foods, and by the personal preferences and reactions to each one of the distinct flavors and aromas.

The ability to develop and harmonize tastes isn't very difficult, but it needs practice. The flavors are constructed based on the sum of all the ingredients that are part of the recipe, from the most to the least important. These produce for us sensations ranging from salty to acidic, sweet, and bitter, in addition to spicy, sour, acrid, refreshing, etc.

Finding a harmony between these sensations is a way of approximating the development of the tastes.

Effect of the following flavors

● **Salty.** It strengthens the flavors. In small proportions it also serves to increase the flavor of sweet dishes. Salt, sea algae, miso, tamari, and celery (lightly) can all produce this effect.

● **Acidic.** Of intense flavor. It lightens and harmonizes the oil in the dish. It complements all the flavors. Examples include lemon, lime, apple vinegar, sauerkraut, and also some that are a little sweeter, like orange and pineapple.

● **Sweet.** It is the natural flavor with the most acceptance, and often appreciated by itself. In the appropriate proportion it combines with all the flavors. Examples include dried fruits, apples, pears, carrots, beets, sweet tomatoes, stevia, and agave.

● **Bitter.** Intense flavor, appropriate only in very specific dishes. In addition to using it on its own, it can be combined with other flavors. It is a light appetite stimulus. Endives, artichokes, grapefruit, and bitter almonds are some examples.

● **Spicy.** It enlivens the dishes and grants them an intense, and at times fine, aroma. It also provides a certain hot taste to recipes. Of course, it should be used in moderation. Examples include garlic, onions, peppers, chili peppers, ginger, and wasabi.

An important element that affects the taste are the oils or fats present in the dish. When we incorporate them, their texture allows many foods to acquire new aspects, in addition to contributing a form of satiation. There are various ingredients that provide grease, including: oils (olive oil, flaxseed oil, walnut oil, sesame oil . . .), dried fruits, avocado, or olives. The combination with sweet flavors and salty flavors is well accepted by the majority of people.

Another significant element is the aromatic herbs and spices. Their use contributes sensations, aromas, and tastes that take us to surprising places.

In choosing ingredients, herbs and spices typical of regions and cultures can be a guide to make a great variety of dishes. For example, with cauliflower (with pine nuts, at times, too) ground as if it had the texture of rice or couscous, we can make the following recipes:

I am the sun (p. 126). Mix the cauliflower with condiments (sesame seeds, tumeric, lemon juice, olive oil, and salt) that take us to the Asiatic zones.

I am sensational (p. 127) (without the avocado). Includes cucumber, soft onion, and tomatoes as the ingredients, in addition to the cauliflower, as well as some condiments (curry, fresh mint, oregano, olive oil, and salt). It offers us typical tastes of the Middle East.

I am a surprise (p. 129). Incorporates some small mushrooms called "Scotch bonnets" and garlic, in addition to basil, olive oil, and salt as condiments. In this case, it offers us tastes that are typically Mediterranean.

I am liberty (p. 128). Add broccoli; red pepper; soft, sweet, raw corn; carrots; and tomatoes, to the following condiments: olive oil, orange juice, garlic, onion, parsley, cumin, salt, and chili pepper, which offer us typical Mexican flavors.

Creams and Soups

Regardless of the time of year, creams and soups constitute an appetizing, nutritious dish. It is ideal to eat them at room temperature, but if we wish for them to be more temperate we can heat up the water to 102.2 degrees Fahrenheit (39 degrees Celsius), in order to avoid destroying the enzymes. If we like cold soup, we will let it sit in the refrigerator for a little while before serving it or we can blend it well with ice.

I am free

Pumpkin cream

3 cups (335 g) of pumpkin • ½ cup (80 g) of mature tomato • ¼ cup (400 g) of apple • 2½ cups (600 ml) of water • 4 teaspoons (20 ml) of olive oil • pepper • salt

1 Peel and throw away the seeds of the pumpkin, cut it up, and set it aside.

2 Peel and remove the seeds from the tomato, cut it up, and set it aside.

3 Peel the apple, cut it up, and set it aside.

4 Put in the vessel of the blender the cut-up pumpkin together with the olive oil, salt, and half of the water, and blend the mixture energetically, until you have a homogenous cream.

5 Continue adding the rest of the ingredients to the cream, except for the pepper, and continue blending.

6 When it's time to serve, sprinkle a pinch of pepper on top.

❋   ❋   ❋   ❋

Optional: The cream will have a very personal touch if upon serving it a pinch of aromatic herbs or a little agave is added in addition to the pepper.

The orange color of the cream awakens a sense of happiness and puts us in a good mood.

Pumpkin
Pumpkin, which is very digestive and feels good in the most delicate stomachs, is especially rich in beta-carotene, vitamin C, vitamin E, flavonoids, and fiber.

I am mysterious

Cream of tomato with olives

For the cream: 5 cups (790 g) of mature tomatoes • 1 ñora pepper • ⅔ cup (95 g) of avocado • 1 cup (115 g) of cucumber • 4 teaspoons (20 ml) of apple vinegar • salt • pepper • **For the garnish:** ¾ cup (150 g) of olives • ⅖ cup (65 g) of peeled tomato and without pips • olive oil • parsley

1 Peel and remove the pips from the tomato.

2 Peel the cucumber and the avocado (and remove the pit).

3 Place the mature tomato, the ñora pepper, the cucumber, the avocado, and the vinegar in the vessel of the blender and blend until you have a homogenous mixture of a fine texture. In the case where the tomatoes aren't peeled, it's recommended to put the cream through a food mill.

4 For the garnish, cut the tomatoes and the olives (de-pitted) into small pieces.

5 Place the cream in a bowl and add the garnish in chunks. Adorn it with a sprig of parsley and a little olive oil.

A cream for the summer. Delicious, refreshing . . . Surprising!

The ñora pepper

This type of pepper—round, of small size, and that has been subjected to a process of drying—contributes to the wide acclaim of a dish due to its strong, original aroma. This quality makes it an exquisite seasoning and is very appreciated, also, for its flavor and the intense coloring that it provides.

I am light

Cucumber soup and vegetables with cream of pine nuts

For the soup: 9⅔ cups (1 kg) of cucumbers • ⅔ cup (90 g) of carrots • 4 teaspoons (20 ml) of lemon juice • ⅓ cup (30 g) of leeks (part white) • ¼ cup (15 g) of dehydrated tomatoes • 4 teaspoons (20 ml) of olive oil • salt • dill • recently ground pepper • **For the cream:** ⅓ cup (50 g) of pine nuts • 3 tablespoons (45 ml) of water • 2 teaspoons (10 ml) of lemon juice • 2 teaspoons (10 ml) of olive oil • salt

To prepare the soup:

1 Soak the tomato for 2 hours.

2 Meanwhile, keep half the cucumber for decoration and peel the rest of it.

3 Place the peeled cucumber in the blender vessel, together with 1 teaspoon of lemon juice, and salt, and blend.

4 Peel the carrots and cut them in very fine slices. Do the same with the half of the cucumber and leeks.

5 Drain the tomatoes and cut them up.

6 Mix in a bowl the carrots, cucumbers, leeks, and the cut tomatoes with the olive oil, salt, 1 teaspoon of lemon juice, and dill. Let it soften for a half hour.

To prepare the cream:

Place all the ingredients in the blender vessel and blend until you have a homogenous cream of fine texture.

To set the plate:

Place the cucumber soup in a bowl. Continue by putting a ration of the macerated vegetables on top and finally sprinkle it with pepper. Accompany it with a portion of the cream of pine nuts.

Refreshing soup for a hot summer night.

Pine nuts

Pine nuts are an excellent food to better the majority of culinary preparations because of their delicate and sweet flavor united with their nutritious richness. They contain proteins, healthy fats, fiber, minerals, and vitamins, in addition to beneficial bioactive substances.

I am energy
Chlorophyll soup

$^1/_{10}$ cup (7 g) of dulse seaweed • ⅛ cup (10 g) of germinated lentils • 3⅓ cup (100 g) of spinach (or you can use chard, cabbage, or lettuce) • ⅜ cup (30 g) of green sprouts of sunflower seeds (or of buckwheat or other kinds of green sprouts) • ⅖ cup (100 ml) of rejuvelac • 3 cups (380 g) of peeled apple • ⅔ cup (95 g) of avocado • 1¾ cup (400 ml) of water

1 Wash the seaweed and drain.

2 Wash the spinach.

3 Place all the ingredients in the blender vessel and blend them very well until getting a mix of a fine and homogenous consistency.

4 It can be served alone or accompanied by almond cream (see recipe **I am laughter**, p. 160), papaya, sauerkraut (see recipe **I am stimulating**, p. 147), or sprouts.

* * * *

Note: This recipe contains the nutrients that the organism needs meet to maintain good health. Easily digestible, depurative, and invigorating, it is recommendable for all, especially for very sick people or convalescents, for its important production of easily assimilable nutrients.

Apples

It is a highly recommended fruit for its nutritious importance. It stands out for its richness of fiber, which favors intestinal circulation, ideal for fighting constipation. In addition, as a part is soluble fiber, it has been shown to regulate cholesterol. It is also considered a blood tonic and a good source of vitamin C. The apple combines well with all greens and produce. In this recipe they can also been substituted for papayas, which will add an important dose of enzymes.

I am potent

Beet cream

2 cups (250 g) of beets • 1½ cup (250 g) of mature tomatoes • ⅓ cup (50 g) of cashews or avocado • 2 cups (500 ml) of water • salt

1 Peel and cut the beets into big pieces.

2 Peel and remove the pips from the tomatoes.

3 Place the cut produce, together with the water, the salt, and the cashews or avocado in the blender vessel and blend.

Note: The type of fat in the cashew nuts or the avocadoes gives this cream a seductive softness that satisfies the palate.

Beets

Beets are rounded roots that have great nutritious value including: sugars, fiber, group B vitamins, potassium, calcium, magnesium, and iodine, in addition to other antioxidants (anthocyanins) responsible for their intense color. Amongst their nutritious virtues they provide depurative, laxative effects.

I am the journey

Noodles

⅛ cup (10 g) of kombu seaweed • 2 tablespoons (35 g) of miso • ½ tablespoon (3 g) dehydrated leek • 2⅓ tablespoons (5 g) yellow dehydrated pepper • 2 tablespoons (5 g) of dehydrated red pepper • 3 tablespoons (10 g) of dehydrated tomato • 1 teaspoon (1⅘ g) of turmeric • 7⅛ cups (890 g) of zucchini • 2¾ cups (650 ml) of water • salt • less than 1 teaspoon (1½ g) curry powder

1 Soak the algae, so that they rehydrate, for 35 minutes.

2 In another tray, dissolve the miso and the turmeric in the water.

3 When the seaweed is rehydrated, drain and cut in pieces.

4 Then cut up the leek, pepper, and dehydrated tomato into small pieces.

5 Continue adding the algae and dehydrated pieces to the water, miso, and turmeric solution and let the mixture rest a minimum of 1 hour.

6 Meanwhile, peel and cut the zucchini in the form of spaghetti. For that, a special machine can be used to make vegetable spaghetti or it can be cut into very fine strips (julienne cut) manually.

7 Salt the zucchini noodles and put them in a colander for 30 minutes so that they lose water. Once they are drained, add the curry.

8 To finish, place the spaghetti in a bowl and add the liquid preparation.

Note: This recipe is inspired by a traditional Japanese soup. The component that gives it the personality is the miso, a fermented food with large nutritious value.

I am presence

Apple cream and avocado with marinated cauliflower

1⅖ cups (120 g) of cauliflower • ⅓ cup (30 g) of celery • 1 garlic clove • ⅔ cup (100 g) of red pepper • 2 cups (270 g) apple • 2 avocadoes • 3⅖ cups (800 ml) of water • 4 tablespoons (60 ml) lemon juice • 4 teaspoons (20 ml) tamari sauce • a pinch of cumin • a pinch of salt • alfalfa sprouts

1 Wash and cut the celery and seedless pepper in small pieces; separate the cauliflower into small flowers.

2 Peel the apples and cut them in pieces. Peel the avocado and garlic. Grate the garlic.

3 Place the cauliflower, celery, garlic, and pepper in a tray. Add half the lemon juice, tamari sauce, and cumin, and mix well. Let the mixture sit for 1 hour.

4 Place the cut up apples, avocado, the rest of the lemon juice, the salt, and the water in the blender vessel and blend well until you obtain a cream with a fine texture.

5 Place the cream in a bowl and, as decoration, add the macerated vegetables together with the alfalfa sprouts.

*   *   *   *

Optional: This cream can also be prepared if you substitute the apples for cucumbers. A good choice would be to prepare it with apple in the winter and with cucumber in the summer.

The soft smell of the cream invites us to slowly taste it to renew our energy.

Cauliflower

This vegetable is an important pantry full of nutrients: provitamin A, vitamin C, potassium, calcium, iron, sulphur, and fiber, in addition to many other bioactive components. Amongst their virtues the following are prominent: their anti-ulcer and anti-diabetic effects, and an antibiotic action from the sulphur compounds that it contains. In addition, the cauliflower, just like the whole cabbage family, fights against constipation and colon cancer, thanks to the important amount of fiber that it offers.

I am valiant

Cream of spinach and fennel

¾ cup (75 g) celery • 6⅓ cups (190 g) spinach • 2 cups (160 g) very soft fennel • 1⅔ cups (275 g) pineapple • 2½ cups (600 ml) water

1 Wash the spinach.

2 Wash and cut the celery and the fennel without the core, in large pieces.

3 Peel the pineapple, extract the core from it, and cut it in big pieces.

4 Place all the ingredients in the blender vessel, add the water, and beat until obtaining a cream with a fine texture.

It is delicious, refreshing, nutritious, and sweet, so that you can savor it slowly.

Fennel

With this leafy, lightly aniseed–flavored veggie, we get this delicious, refreshing soup, which is also at the same time nutritious. If the fennel used isn't very soft, it is advised to put the mixture through the blender. Amongst its virtues is facilitating the digestive process, helping to eliminate the intestinal gases, and being a light laxative.

I am penetrating

Carrot soup

1⅛ cups (150 g) carrots • 2 teaspoons (10 ml) lemon juice • 2½ teaspoon (5 g) ginger • ⅔ cup (80 g) tomatoes • 4 tablespoons (15 g) dehydrated tomatoes • 1 cup (150 g) apples • 2 teaspoons (10 ml) olive oil • 3 cups (700 ml) water • salt • pepper

1 Soak the dehydrated tomatoes in water for an hour.

2 Meanwhile, peel and cut up the carrots and the apples. Peel the tomatoes and depip them.

3 Put half the water together with the cut-up carrots, lemon juice, olive oil, and salt in the blender vessel, and blend the mixture well until it becomes a cream.

4 Continue adding the rest of the water, the tomato, the ginger, and the dehydrated tomatoes, and beat it again.

5 Finally, add the apple to the mixture and blend until you obtain a homogenous cream, of a fine texture.

6 Place the soup in a dish and sprinkle pepper on top.

Following these instructions cautiously, you can obtain a delicious preparation with an elegant texture.

Carrots

It is a vegetable with a light, sweet flavor, whose best nutritious attribute is its great abundance of carotene, with a large amount of water content. The minerals, vitamins, and fiber stand out amongst its nutrients. Amongst its minerals, the following stand out: calcium, iron, potassium, and phosphorus. The predominant vitamins are: B1, B2, C, and E.

I am sweet

Papaya cream

1½ cups (200 g) papaya • 3¾ cups (600 g) tomatoes • 1¾ cups (400 ml) water • 2 teaspoons (10 ml) olive oil • salt • **To adorn:** ⅓ cup (55 g) onion • basil

1 Peel the papaya, take out the seeds, and grind it up.

2 Peel the tomato, take out the pips, and grind it up.

3 Peel the onion.

4 Place the papaya and the ground tomatoes in the blender vessel, together with the water, salt, and olive oil. Blend the mixture until you get a cream with a fine consistency.

5 Place the cream in a dish and decorate it with the onion and basil, cut very fine.

A palm tree, a tropical beach … What do you discover when capturing it?

Papaya

This tropical fruit contains a great amount of enzymes, minerals, and vitamins. In it we can emphasize, for its importance, the enzyme known as "papain," which effectively contributes to the digestion of the proteins.

I am recognition

Mango cream

6 cups (1 kg) mango (approximately 2 large mangoes) • ⅓ cup (50 g) pineapples • 1¾ cup (400 ml) water • 1 tablespoon (4 g) of fresh mint

1 Peel the mangoes and put aside the pits.

2 Place all the ingredients, except the mint, in the blender vessel, and blend continually until you get a cream.

3 Chop the mint very fine and sprinkle it over the bowls just before serving.

Note: This soup, sweet and refreshing, can be eaten as a dessert.

Mango

Delicious fruit, with a soft texture and a sweet, delicate flavor that reminds us of a peach or an apricot. It offers a large amount of carotenoids (provitamin A) and vitamins C and E, in addition to those from group B (especially pholates). Amongst the minerals that it contains, we should emphasize the potassium. It also possesses diverse antioxidant components. This explains all its virtues: it contributes to the good state of the skin and vision, it prevents cardiovascular problems and early aging, and it has diuretic and laxative effects.

I am authenticity

Green cream

1 cup (145 g) peeled pepper • 1⅕ cups (120 g) celery stalk • 1⅔ cup (275 g) pineapple without the skin or core • 1⅔ cups (50 g) spinach • 2 cups (270 g) apples • ½ avocado • 2 cups (½ l) water

1 Cut the pepper, pineapple, and celery into pieces.

2 Peel the apple and grind it.

3 Wash and drain the spinach.

4 Peel the avocado and take out the pit.

5 Put all the ingredients in the blender vessel and blend them until you get a cream with a uniform texture.

Note: This is a sweet cream that offers an important dose of vitamins, minerals, proteins, vegetable oil (85 percent of which are unsaturated, which is to say, with beneficial effects relating to the levels of cholesterol in the blood and the state of the arteries and the heart), antioxidants, and fiber. It is an important food for the whole organism.

This recipe fills our body with chlorophyll and solar light.

I am excellent

Pineapple cream with pine nut milk and marinated asparagus

7¼ cups (1⅓ kg) pineapple • 3 tablespoons (6 g) fresh ginger • salt • pepper • **For the pine nut milk:** ⅓ cup (50 g) pine nuts • 1¼ cup (300 ml) water • **For the marinated asparagus:** 2¼ cups (300 g) asparagus • ⅓ cup (50 g) soft onion • 4 teaspoons (20 ml) olive oil • 4 teaspoons (20 ml) tamari

1 Peel the pineapple, take out the core, and cut it into pieces.

2 In the blender vessel, blend the pineapple with the pine nut milk and the ginger.

3 Pass that liquid through a Chinese colander.

4 Place the cream in a dish with some asparagus in the middle. Season to your liking.

To make the pine nut milk:

1 Soak the pine nuts for 2 hours.

2 Once time has passed, drain them and blend them with the water.

To make the marinated asparagus:

1 Separate the hard part of the asparagus; wash and layer it using a vegetable peeler.

2 Peel the onion and cut it (julienne cut).

3 Place the asparagus on a tray, together with the onion, olive oil, and tamari sauce, and let it soften for a half an hour.

Creamy, sweet, and spicy mix of flavors.

Salads

The explosion of colors, textures, and flavors that the ingredients in salad offers creates a very attractive display. It also creates a dish that is delicious and provides a great source of nutrients. Once the components have been combined, each salad can be varied as desired. Just don't forget that good decoration and color are two key requisites for whetting the appetite. Here we show you a bunch.

I am happy
Greek salad

4 cups (650 g) tomatoes • 1 cup (160 g) red pepper • ⅓ cup (40 g) green pepper • ½ cup (85 g) black olives • ⅔ cup (100 g) soft onion • 2⅓ cups (230 g) cucumber • 4 to 5 teaspoons (2½ g) fresh parsley • 2 teaspoons (10 g) of dry thyme • 4 teaspoons (20 ml) lemon juice • 4 teaspoons (20 ml) olive oil • seed cheese • salt

1 Peel and remove the seeds from the tomatoes.

2 Peel the onion.

3 Wash the peppers and cucumber.

4 Take out the seeds from the peppers.

5 Cut all the ingredients into pieces.

6 Place the cut up produce in a salad bowl and season them with the lemon juice, olive oil, thyme, and salt.

7 Just before serving, add the parsley leaves, cheese, and olives.

To dance… this is that which reminds us of this salad's taste.

Peppers

This vegetable is an exceptional source of vitamin C. It also provides vitamin A, vitamin B2, flavonoids, vitamin E, and fewer amounts of the majority of minerals and fiber. It is a vegetable that is favorable to digestion as it activates the separation of gastric juices, and it acts as a gentle laxative and as a potent anti-inflammatory and protector of the circulatory system.

I am strong

Fennel salad

3 cups (300 g) of fennel • ⅓ cup (50 g) of red pepper • ½ teaspoon (2½ ml) of tumeric • 1 cup (150 g) of avocado • 2 teaspoons (10 ml) lime juice • salt

1 Wash and layer the fennel finely without the core.

2 Wash the pepper, peel the avocado, and take out the pit.

3 Cut the pepper (without seeds) and avocado in small squares.

4 Place the ingredients in a bowl, add the lime juice, tumeric, and salt, and mix it all well.

The aniseed-flavored fennel with the tumeric is like a delicious sigh . . .

I am decision

Cabbage salad

5 cups (½ kg) green cabbage • 1 cup (100 g) purple cabbage • 4 cups (600 g) tomatoes • ⅛ cup (5 g) fresh ginger • 7 cloves (25 g) garlic • 2 avocadoes • 1 tablespoon (15ml) extra virgin olive oil • 4 teaspoons (20 ml) lemon or lime juice • salt (optional)

1 Peel, take out the pips, and cut the tomatoes.

2 Cut the green and purple cabbage very fine and save it. The best machine to use to grate it is a food processor, but if you don't have one, it can be done manually with a mandolin, for example.

3 Peel, remove the pit from, and dice the avocadoes.

4 Place the green cabbage, purple cabbage, extra virgin olive oil, lemon juice, salt, and avocadoes on a tray.

5 Grate the ginger and peel and mince the garlic. Add them to the rest of the ingredients. Mix all well. You can also do it with your hands. In this way, the fiber of the cabbage is broken lightly and allows the oil from the avocado and the condiments to mix better. Do it with love.

6 Add the tomatoes and mix lightly.

Divine cabbage … freshness and softness!

Cabbage

The great nutritional value of this family (which includes broccoli, purple cabbage, cabbage, cauliflower, and Brussels sprouts) is not only due to its high vitamin and mineral content, but rather a whole series of substances with antioxidants and anti-carcinogen effects: a notable consumption of cabbage can reduce the incidence of colon, rectal, and thyroid cancer. In addition, cabbages are a great source of fiber, are low in calories, and resist low temperatures. Another virtue of this family is that, to the contrary of other vegetables, they are notable sources of iodine and selenium.

I am tolerant

Endive boats

2 endives • 3 tablespoons (45 ml) lime juice • ⅓ cup (50 g) onion • 3 cups (300 g) cucumber • 1⅓ cups (170 g) zucchini • 1 small carrot • salt • **For the cream:** 8 teaspoons (40 ml) of tamari • ⅔ cup (100 g) of cashews

1 Peel and dice the cucumber and onion and marinate for ½ hour with the lime juice and salt.

2 Peel and dice the zucchini.

3 Peel and cut the carrot into very fine strips.

4 Mix the cucumber, onion, and zucchini with the cream.

5 Separate the endive leaves and fill them with the aforementioned mix. Adorn it with the fine carrot strips.

To prepare the cream:

1 Soak the cashews for 2 hours. After that, drain them.

2 Blend the cashews with the tamari and water, until it looks like a thick cream.

Navigate with its flavors.

I am succulence

Cucumber and soft onion salad

9 cups (900 g) cucumber • ⅔ cup (95 g) soft onion • less than 1 teaspoon (⅘ g) dry dill • salt • **For the cream:** ⅓ cup (50 g) cashews • ¹⁄₁₀ teaspoon (.45 ml) lemon juice • 3 tablespoons (9 g) dehydrated tomatoes • 5 tablespoons (70 ml) water • 4 teaspoons (20 ml) olive oil • salt

1 Wash and cut the cucumbers in slices, salt them, and let them drain for ½ hour. If you want, peel them before cutting them.

2 Peel the softened onions and cut them very fine.

3 Add the cut onion to the cream and mix gently.

4 In a dish, place the cucumber slices in circles, scatter on top of the cream, and, finally, sprinkle with the dill.

To prepare the cream:

1 Soak the dehydrated tomatoes for 1 hour.

2 Once soaked, drain them well. Afterward, place them in the blender together with the dried fruits, lemon juice, water, olive oil, and salt, and blend until you get a cream of fluid consistency.

A simple recipe … but very juicy.

Dill

The ancient settlers of Egypt, Greece, and Rome used this magnificent aromatic plant, as much for its gastronomic properties as for its therapeutic ones. The leaves and seeds are used (ground in the case of using them in salads) to make vinegarettes and marinades. Amongst its virtues we can emphasize its carminative (prevents the formation of intestinal gases) and diuretic effects and its ability to serve as a good appetizer food.

I am a marvel

Mango and watercress salad

1 bunch watercress • 5¾ cups (950 g) mangoes • 1 lettuce head • ⅓ cup (40 g) walnuts • 2 tablespoons (7 g) purple onion • **To make the dressing:** • 1 teaspoon (5 ml) lemon juice • ⅖ cup (100 ml) olive oil • sprinkle ($^7/_{10}$ g) of mustard powder • sprinkle (1 g) of minced garlic • splash (11 ml) of agave • a pinch of pepper • salt

1 Soak the walnuts for ½ hour. Once this time has passed, drain them and set them aside.

2 Wash the watercress, drain them well, and set them aside.

3 Peel the mango and cut it into pieces.

4 Peel and cut the onion into very fine slices and set aside.

5 Mix the dressing with the onion, mango, and walnuts, and let it marinade for ½ hour.

6 Place on the dish, as a base, the lettuce and watercress, and add the marinade on top.

To make the dressing:
Place the lemon juice, olive oil, mustard, minced garlic, agave, salt, and pepper, in a bowl, beat energetically with a fork until it's homogenized.

A very exotic recipe … Enjoy it!

Watercress

They are plants that grow spontaneously and locally habitually close to fountains or streams. In the past the watercress was cast aside as food and nowadays it is very highly regarded, including in this author's cooking. Watercress offers a great amount of antioxidants and folic acid, in addition to sulfur compounds and abundant fiber, which helps to combat constipation. For all of these reasons, this veggie is digestive, depurative, invigorating, and expectorant.

I am a voyage

Boat of germinated foods

1¼ cup (100 g) lettuce • 3 cups (470 g) tomato • 5 cups (500 g) cucumber • ¾ cup (115 g) red pepper • ⅝ cup (90 g) soft onion • 4 teaspoons (3½ g) fresh basil • germinated alfalfa • **For the sauce:** 3 tablespoons (45 ml) lemon juice • 2 teaspoons (10 ml) agave • 4 tablespoons (60 ml) olive oil • 2 teaspoons (15 ml) of tamari • salt • pepper

1 Peel and cut the cucumbers into small pieces.

2 Peel and remove the pips from the tomatoes, and cut them into small pieces.

3 Wash and cut the pepper into small pieces.

4 Peel the softened onion and cut it into small pieces.

5 Place the cut up veggies in a bowl, add the fresh, minced basil, and salt it. Let it marinate for ½ hour.

6 Roll the sheets of lettuce with the vegetable mixture, as if they were boats.

7 Lastly, add the germinated foods on top.

To make the sauce:
Mix all the ingredients at once and beat them with a fork until you have a homogenous sauce.

Note: The combination of the grease (from the olive oil) with the mixture of salted, sweet, and acidic flavors makes for a delicious sensation for the palate.

Lettuce

Popular green-leafed vegetable, and, thus, a chlorophyll provider, lettuce contains an elevated proportion of water. Its significant portion of provitamin A, vitamin C, potassium, and calcium, in addition to other bioactive substances, should also be mentioned amongst those that stand out for their sedative effects. Their habitual consumption can produce a sense of relaxation.

I am opportunity

Turnip and celery salad with seaweed

4 tablespoons (28 g) dried hijiki seaweed • ¾ cup (72 g) celery • 1¾ cups (230 g) turnip • ½ cup (84 g) soft onion • ⅘ cup (150 g) tomato • 2½ tablespoons (10 g) parsley • sprinkle (1 g) of thyme • 5 tablespoons (80 ml) lemon or lime juice • 4 teaspoons (50 ml) tamari • 2 tablespoons (30 ml) olive oil

1 Soak the seaweed for ½ hour.

2 Drain the seaweed, put it in a bowl, and mix with the tamari, olive oil, and lemon juice. Let marinade for another ½ hour.

3 Peel and remove the pips from the tomato, and cut it into pieces.

4 Peel the onion and turnip, and cut them, julienne style.

5 Wash and cut the celery, julienne style.

6 Once the veggies are cut, place them in a salad bowl, mix them well, and add the minced parsley and thyme.

7 Add the seaweed to the vegetables and let it soften to your taste.

A root, a vegetable of the sea . . .
A magnificent combination.

Celery

The refreshing quality of the crunchy celery makes it very appropriate to include in many salads. It has good qualities for an appetizer, to stimulate the secretion of saliva and the gastric juices. It is a fountainhead of fiber, vitamins, mineral salts, and other substances, most prominently the essential oil it contains, responsible for the majority of its therapeutic properties. It is an excellent depurative and diuretic, which is recommended in many weight-reduction diets.

I am joyful

Dehydrated tomato and black olive salad

1½ cups (80 g) dehydrated tomatoes • ¾ cup (150 g) olives • ⅛ cup (25 g) soft onion • ¼ cup (35 g) red pepper • 2 teaspoons (10 ml) olive oil • 1 teaspoon (5 ml) tamari • 2 teaspoons (10 ml) lemon juice • 1 teaspoon (1⅓ g) dried oregano • head of lettuce

1 Soak the dehydrated tomatoes for 1 hour.

2 Drain and cut them in fine pieces.

3 De-pit and cut up the olives.

4 Peel and mince the onion.

5 Wash and cut the pepper without seeds in fine pieces.

6 On a tray, mix the olive oil, lemon juice, tamari, and oregano with the rest of the ingredients, except the lettuce. Let the mixture settle for at least ½ hour.

7 Wash and cut the lettuce to your liking and mix it with the preparation.

❊   ❊   ❊   ❊

Optional: This salad is delicious if you add 1 spoonful of cashew cheese to each plate (see recipe *I am a dancer*, p. 162).

Olives

A fruit that is characterized by its large content of monosaturated good fats and fiber. The quantity of fats, without a doubt, can vary according to the type of olive and its state of maturation. All of them contain vitamin E and polyphenols, both of which have a noticeable antioxidant effect. It is an ingredient with a multitude of culinary options.

I am profundity

Kohlrabi salad

6⅔ cups (950 g) kohlrabi • **For the sauce:** ⅓ cup (50 g) cashews • 3⅓ tablespoons (50 ml) olive oil • ⅔ cup (100 ml) water • 2 teaspoons (10 ml) lemon juice • 1 teaspoon (4½ g) mustard powder • salt

1   Peel the kohlrabi and grate it delicately.

2   Add it to the sauce, mix it well, and let it settle for 30 minutes.

To prepare the sauce:

1   Soak the cashews for 6 hours and drain them.

2   Add the rest of the ingredients to the cashews and blend until you have a fine cream.

A salad bowl full of nutrients.

Cashews

The same as the rest of the dried fruit and nuts, cashews contain a high proportion of fat. Thus, it has the power to energize and, consequently, does well during the growing stage for athletes whose activities are intense. It also stands out for its abundant production of magnesium, an essential mineral for the numerous processes and chemical reactions of the body, proteins, vitamins, and diverse bioactive components.

I am life

Beets and sprouts salad

3 cups (400 g) beets • 1½ cups (100 g) lentil sprouts • 2½ cups (400 g) tomatoes • ⅔ cup (100 g) red peppers • ½ cup (85 g) soft onion • ¾ cup (85 g) of radishes • **For the dressing:** 4 teaspoons (20 ml) olive oil • 4 teaspoons (20 ml) lemon juice • a sprinkle (2 g) salt • 2 tablespoons (6 g) fresh oregano

1 Peel and remove the pips from the tomatoes and cut them into thin strips.

2 Wash and cut the pepper without seeds and the radishes in thin strips.

3 Peel and grate the beets.

4 Peel and cut the soft onion, julienne style.

5 Place the cut vegetables in a salad bowl and add the sprouts and dressing. Mix and let it marinade for ½ hour.

To prepare the dressing:
Mix the oil, lemon juice, salt, and fresh minced oregano energetically.

A salad full of energy!

I am vigor
Vegetable stew

3¼ cups (430 g) kohlrabi • 3 cups (250 g) carrots • 3 cups (380 g) apples • ⅛ cup (20 g) raisins • ⅓ cup (40 g) sunflower seeds • **For the sauce:** less than 1 teaspoon (1 g) of cumin • 4 teaspoons (20 ml) olive oil • 2 teaspoons (10 ml) tamari • 2 teaspoons (6 g) garlic • 4 teaspoons (20 ml) lemon juice

1 Soak the sunflower seeds for 6 hours; then drain.

2 Peel the kohlrabi, carrots, and apples, and cut them julienne style.

3 Mix the sunflower seeds, raisins, kohlrabi, carrots, and apples in a bowl and add the sauce. Let it marinade for ½ hour.

To prepare the sauce:
Place the olive oil, tamari, peeled and minced garlic, lemon juice, and cumin in a bowl, and beat energetically with a fork until you get a homogenous sauce.

Raisins

Raisins come via the process of desiccating grapes. Different methods have been used, from simply exposing them to the sun, to automatic industrial processes. They produce a lot of energy and, like fresh grapes, we are rewarded with help maintaining good veins and arteries (primarily the coronary arteries). Other important properties are: they're antianemic and contain antioxidants, anticarcinogens, and laxatives.

I am just

Radish and soft spinach salad

3½ cups (450 g) radishes • 1⅔ cups (200 g) apples • ½ cup (100 g) black olives • 6 cups (200 g) very soft, small-leafed spinach • **For the dressing:** 3 tablespoons (40 ml) olive oil • 2 tablespoons (6 g) fresh oregano • 2 teaspoons (10 ml) lemon juice • salt

1 Wash the radishes and grate them delicately.

2 Wash and peel the apples and grate them finely.

3 Mix the radishes and apples in the dressing.

4 Remove the pits from the olives and chop them.

5 Wash the spinach and drain them.

6 Distribute the mixture of radish and apple over the spinach and scatter the olives on top.

To make the dressing:
Chop the oregano; place it in a bowl together with the olive oil, lemon juice, and salt. Beat energetically with a fork.

I am fluidity

Arugula and orange salad with red pepper sauce

10 cups (200 g) arugula • 4 oranges • ¼ cup (50 g) black olives • **For the sauce:** 1⅓ cups (200 g) red peppers • ½ cup (30 g) dehydrated tomatoes • 2 teaspoons mustard • 1 clove garlic • less than 1 teaspoon (3 g) fresh ginger root • 4 teaspoons (20 ml) olive oil • salt

1 Remove the pits from the olives, cut them into small pieces, and set them aside.

2 Peel the oranges, to the edge, careful that none of the white skin remains, and cut them in small, fine pieces.

3 Place the orange slices above the arugula and, finally, scatter the olives and sauce on top of the salad.

To prepare the sauce:

1 Soak the dehydrated tomatoes in water for 1 hour.

2 Wash the peppers and extract the seeds.

3 Peel the garlic.

4 After the soaking time has terminated, drain the tomatoes, place them in the blender vessel, together with the rest of the sauce's ingredients, and blend them until you have a homogenous cream. Set it aside.

* * * *

Note: This appetizing salad can have an excellent alternative upon adding to it a portion of soft onion, previously marinated in olive oil and salt for ½ hour.

Arugula

This wild plant is very widespread in the Mediterranean region and very easy to grow. It contains a notable quantity of vitamin C. Digestive properties are also attributed to this plant. Its peculiar taste creates a very useful appeal in order to heighten our repertoire of salads and other dishes.

Assorted Dishes

The following dishes create experiences that enlighten your imagination and creativity. As much in their production as in their presentation, in addition to being intriguing, they are delicious.

I am ecstasy

"Torn" Tomato

9⅓ cups (1½ kg) mature, thick tomatoes • 1½ avocadoes • ⅜ cup (15 g) fresh basil • 2 teaspoons (6 g) garlic • salt • olive oil

1 Peel the tomatoes and take out the pips. After, cut them with your fingers into strips and place them on a plate.

2 Peel the garlic. Grate it or overlay it.

3 Add the garlic to the tomatoes together with the minced basil, and let it marinate for 1 hour.

4 Once the time has passed, peel the avocadoes, put aside the pit, cut them into pieces, and add them to the tomatoes with extreme caution so they don't break.

5 Upon serving, add the olive oil and salt. Once this is done, make sure the tomato doesn't dry out.

✳ ✳ ✳ ✳

Note: As an optional alternative, the garlic can be substituted for onion, but then it's advised to marinate it earlier with the salt and olive oil and add it also upon serving.

The bright red of this feast brings us strength and courage.

Tomato

This popular ingredient, with its large amount of varieties, offers us an abundance of vitamin C, as well as beta-carotene and other carotenoids that serve as antioxidants, in its fresh state. It also provides minerals like potassium, magnesium, and calcium. It is a form of produce whose habitual ingestion contributes to cardiovascular protection and protection from premature aging, in addition to being depurative and a diuretic.

I am tenderness

Marinated artichokes

2.2 pounds (1 kg) artichokes • ⅙ cup (10 g) fresh parsley • **For the seasoning:** 1½ tablespoons (20 g) garlic • ⅗ teaspoon (2 g) dried artichoke • 3 tablespoons (40 ml) lemon juice • 2 tablespoons (30 ml) olive oil • 1 tablespoon (15 ml) tamari

1 Get rid of the external leaves of the artichokes until only the hearts are left.

2 Cut the hearts into very fine layers and add them to a tray with the seasoning.

3 Macerate them for a minimum of 2 hours.

4 When serving, chop the parsley finely and sprinkle it on top.

To make the seasoning:

1 Peel the garlic, overlay it, and place it in a bowl with the chopped artichoke, lemon juice, olive oil, and tamari.

2 Mix the ingredients with a fork until they're homogenized.

Note: The marinated artichokes can be served accompanied by small bits of tomato, peeled, pips removed, and previously seasoned.

A recipe that allows you to taste the true flavor of soft artichokes.

Artichokes

With a notable content of carbohydrates and fiber, practically without fats, it also provides group B vitamins (mainly B1—thiamine—and B3—niacin) and minerals like potassium, sodium, magnesium, and calcium. Their therapeutic qualities are determined, in great measure, by various substances that are found in small amounts amongst their composition. It is recommended for its beneficial actions on the intestinal, hepatic, and biliary functions, in addition to acting effectively as a diuretic.

I am spectacular

Marinated eggplant

2.5 cups (350 g) eggplant • 1¼ cups (160 g) carrot • ⅔ cups (100 g) red pepper • ¼ cup (50 g) black olives • ⅔ cup (100 g) onion • 1 tablespoon (15 ml) lemon juice • 4 tablespoons (60 ml) olive oil • 1 tablespoon (4 g) fresh oregano • less than 1 teaspoon (4 g) salt

1 Peel the eggplant and cut it in fine strips.

2 Peel and cut the carrot in fine layers.

3 Place the two cut vegetables on a tray, add the lemon juice, olive oil, oregano, and a sprinkle of salt (2 g) and let it marinade all night.

4 Peel and cut the onion in fine strips and let it macerate with a sprinkle (2 g) of salt for 30 minutes.

5 Wash the pepper and put aside its seeds. Cut it julienne style and mix it with the marinated strips of eggplant and carrot.

6 Add the onion to the previous preparation.

7 Remove the pits and chop the olives and upon serving mix them with the rest of the ingredients.

It is an ideal recipe to discover the spectacular flavor of the eggplant.

Eggplant

Eggplant is rich in fiber, which helps with intestinal movement. It also contains terpenes, substances capable of neutralizing the effect of the steroid hormones and potassium, which helps to regulate the arterial pressure. It barely contains any fats and has very few calories. Other principal properties are: stimulates the digestive process, favors diuresis, and reduces cholesterol levels.

I am alliance

Edible seaweed with chimichurri

½ cup (40 g) edible seaweed • **For the seasoning:** ⅛ tablespoon (2 g) chimichurri sauce • sprinkle (½ gram) of thyme • 2 teaspoons (10 ml) lemon juice • 1 tablespoon (15 ml) olive oil • salt

1 Soak the seaweed all night.

2 The next morning, drain them and mix them with the seasoning.

To prepare the seasoning:
Put the olive oil, lemon juice, chimichurri, thyme, and salt in a bowl, and beat energetically. Let it rest ½ hour so the condiments are well mixed together. Stir.

I am friendship

Edible seaweed with basil mayonnaise

⅓ cup (40 g) edible seaweed • **For the mayonnaise:** ⅓ cup (60 g) cashews • ⅕ cup (3½ grams) of basil • 5 teaspoons (25 ml) olive oil • 4 tablespoons (60 ml) water • salt

1 Soak the seaweed all night.

2 The next morning, drain them and mix them with the mayonnaise.

To prepare the mayonnaise:
Soak the cashews for 6 hours. Drain them and blend them with the rest of the ingredients until obtaining a sauce with a texture similar to the mayonnaise.

I am diversion

Marinated Asparagus

A bundle of asparagus (about 2½ cups or 330 g) • **For the seasoning:** 3 tablespoon (10 g) ginger • 2 teaspoons (5 g) garlic • 4 teaspoons (20 ml) olive oil • 1 teaspoon (5 ml) agave • 1 teaspoon (5 ml) rice vinegar • 3 teaspoons (1.5 g) dry tarragon • a pinch of salt

1 Remove the hard part of the asparagus, wash them, and cut them lengthways in half.

2 Place them on a tray together with the seasoning and let it marinate for a night.

To make the seasoning:

1 Peel the garlic and cut it in layers.

2 Grate the ginger.

3 Put the olive oil, agave, vinegar, tarragon, garlic, ginger, and salt in a bowl. Beat it with a fork.

A soft, delicious mouthful to taste before the main foods.

Asaparagus

Asparagus is a very popular vegetable, with a great proportion of water and minimal fats. It provides very few calories in the diet, a quality that makes it especially helpful in weight-loss diets. It is rich in nutrients like: potassium, phosophorus, provitamin A, vitamin C, folic acid, and fiber. Fiber contributes to the sense of satiation, while at the same time offering laxative effects. It also has diuretic effects.

I am elegance
Carrot Carpaccio

3⅕ cups (400 g) carrots • ½ cup (100 g) olives • ⅛ cup (4 g) parsley • 2 teaspoon (6 g) soaked, drained sesame seeds • **For the dressing:** 3 tablespoons (40 ml) sesame oil • 3 tablespoons (40 ml) lemon juice • 2 teaspoons (10 ml) of agave • salt • pepper

1 Remove the pits from the olives and chop them well into tiny pieces.

2 Peel the carrots and grate them with the vegetable peeler into very fine pieces.

3 Add the seasoning and sesame seeds to the carrots, and let it marinate for a minimum of 30 minutes.

4 Past the marinating time, add the olives and parsley (cut very small) and serve it promptly.

To prepare the dressing:
Mix the sesame oil, olive oil, lemon juice, agave, salt, and pepper.

Quick to prepare, easy to eat, and elegant in its presentation.

Sesame oil

Obtained from the sesame seeds, it is recommended to use it cold-pressed and without refining. It provides an interesting flavor to dressings and sauces. It is rich in minerals, especially calcium, iron, and zinc; vitamins B and E, as well as unsaturated fatty acids (rich in omega-6) and other elements. Amongst its properties, it reduces cholesterol levels, improves the nervous system functions, and decreases rheumatic issues. It is also used in beauty treatments for its ability to hydrate the skin, and other uses.

I am an abundance

Cultivated oyster mushroom pastries in pesto

3½ cups (300 g) cultivated oyster mushrooms (*Pleurotus Euringuis*) • **For the pesto:** 5 tablespoons (75 ml) olive oil • 4 teaspoons (20 g) pine nuts • ¾ cup (17 g) fresh basil • 1 teaspoon (1 g) fresh oregano • 1 teaspoon (½ g) fresh sage • 1 teaspoon (3 g) garlic • salt

1 Clean the mushrooms and slice them or overlay them very finely.

2 Spread the pieces of mushrooms with pesto and arrange them on top of one another until they have formed a puffed pastry. Save it in the fridge all night.

To prepare the pesto:

1 Peel the garlic.

2 Blend all the ingredients until you have a uniform sauce.

With the pastries, the texture and flavor of the mushrooms have been transformed into an exquisite bite of paradise.

I am cooperation

Marinated shitake mushrooms with dulse leaf flakes

3 cups (300 g) shitake mushrooms • 5 tablespoons (80 ml) olive oil • 2 teaspoons (10 ml) lemon juice • 1 tablespoon (7 g) dulse leaf flakes • a pinch of pepper • a pinch of dry thyme • salt

1 Separate the trunks from the mushrooms.

2 Clean the heads and cut them in strips a finger in thickness.

3 Place them on a tray, add the olive oil, lemon juice, dulse leaf flakes, pepper, thyme, and salt; mix it all well.

4 Let them macerate for 2 hours.

5 To finish (this is optional), dehydrate the macerated mushrooms for ½ hour.

※　※　※　※

Note: These delicious mushrooms seem to have been cooked, but since in reality they are raw, conserve all their energy and lightness. They can be served at lukewarm temperature from the dehydrator as a delicious appetizer to nibble or as a side dish to many main courses.

I am luminosity

Blood orange marinated champignon mushrooms

5½ cups (500 g) champignon mushrooms • **Condiments for the marinade:** 3 tablespoons (40 ml) lemon juice • 3 tablespoons (40 ml) olive oil • 3 tablespoons (40 ml) blood orange juice • 1 teaspoon (4 g) mustard powder • 1 teaspoonful agave tea • **For the stuffing:** ½ cup (75 g) onion • ⅔ cup (100 g) red pepper • ⅘ cup (140 g) orange • 2 teaspoons (10 ml) olive oil • sprinkle (½ g) of thyme • salt • pepper

1 Separate the bottom from the head of the mushrooms.

2 Clean the heads and marinate them overnight with the condiments.

3 Drain them and add the stuffing to the interior.

To prepare the condiments for the marinade

1 Place the blood orange juice, lemon juice, olive oil, mustard powder, and agave on a tray.

2 Beat with a fork until the mixture is well homogenized.

To prepare the ingredients for the stuffing:

1 Wash and cut the pepper without seeds into small pieces.

2 Peel and cut the onion into small pieces.

3 Peel the orange to the edge and cut it in very small pieces.

4 Place the pepper, onion, orange, thyme, and olive oil on a tray, and add salt and pepper according to taste. Let it marinate for 1 hour.

The blood oranges dye the mushrooms, giving them luminosity, freshness, and vigor. We will note their vitality at the first bite.

Champignon Mushroom

This mushroom, with anti-diabetic effects, helps make all kinds of dishes. It has a cap, ring, and stem of whitish tones and with chocolate-colored layers (get rid of those with very dark layers). Its flesh is white, consistent, and of a very pleasant taste and aroma. The mushrooms usually eaten are cultivated.

I am truth

Seaweed tartare

⅓ cup (25 g) wakame seaweed • ⅓ cup (25 g) dulse leaf flakes • ⅓ cup (50 g) onion • 2 teaspoons (7 g) garlic • 1 cup (250 ml) orange juice • 3 teaspoons (15 g) fresh ginger • ½ cup (60 g) capers

1 Soak the wakame and dulse for 30 minutes in water and then drain them.

2 Cut them into small pieces and place them on a tray.

3 Peel and chop the onion and garlic into small pieces.

4 Grate the ginger.

5 On another tray, mix the onion, garlic, and ginger with the orange juice.

6 Pour this mixture on top of the wakame and dulse and let it sit for about 2 hours in the fridge.

7 Before serving, add the capers.

Sea vegetables, source of nutrients.

Wakame seaweed

Its fine flavor makes it very appropriate for a varied number of dishes. It contains a great proportion of fiber and protein, and a very little amount of fat. Its great remineralizing ability is supported by its important contribution of minerals: magnesium, calcium, potassium, iron, and trace elements like zinc, selenium, manganese, boron, cobalt, copper, and vanadium. Amongst all of those, calcium stands out (it provides a lot more than milk). Its contribution of nutrients is complemented by vitamins A, B1, B2, and C. Wakame is recommended for its depurative effects and it is advised against in the case of those who suffer from a thyroid condition, due to its high iodine content.

I am inspiration

Small heaps of guacamole and tomato with slices of zucchini and alfalfa sprouts

For the slices: 2½ cups (315 g) zucchini • salt • **For the tomato:** 2½ cups (410 g) tomato • 1 teaspoon (5 ml) olive oil • less than 1 teaspoon (1.5 g) garlic • salt • **For the guacamole:** sprinkle (.6 g) dry basil • 1 cup (170 g) of avocado • ¼ cup (35 g) red pepper • ¼ cup (45 g) onion • 1 teaspoon (5 ml) olive oil • splash of (3 ml) tamari • less than 1 teaspoon (.6 g) garlic • salt • chile pepper • **To decorate:** alfalfa sprouts • **For the olive oil aromatized by basil:** 4 teaspoons (20 ml) olive oil • sprinkle (1 g) of dry basil • salt

To prepare the slices:

1 Peel the zucchini and cut it in round slices.

2 Salt them and marinade at least 30 minutes, so that they lose the water.

To prepare the tomato:

1 Peel the tomato, take out the pips, and cut into small pieces.

2 Marinade it with (5 ml) of olive oil, salt, and less than 1 teaspoon (1.5 g) of garlic, a minimum of 30 minutes.

To prepare the guacamole:

1 Wash and cut the red pepper into tiny pieces.

2 Peel and chop the onion into very small pieces.

3 Peel the garlic and grate it.

4 Peel and remove the pit from the avocado, place it on a tray, and, with a fork, make a puree. Add the onion, pepper, olive oil, tamari, garlic, basil, salt, and red pepper, and mix.

To prepare the mounds:

1 In a baseless mold, place a slice of zucchini, followed by a little bit of marinated tomato. Prepare another slice of zucchini, a little bit of guacamole, and another slice of zucchini.

2 Remove the mold, put a handful of alfalfa sprouts on it, and season with basil oil: put all the ingredients in a bowl, beat energetically with a fork, and let it rest.

A dream of sweetness for its aroma and flavor.

Alfalfa sprouts

They are a great source of amino acids, enzymes, carbohydrates, flavonoids, chlorophyll, and fiber. In addition, they contain vitamins C, B9 (folic acid), provitamin A (beta-carotene), E, and K. To top it all, they have an interesting re-mineralizing effect on account of its varied portion of minerals, such as potassium, magnesium, calcium, iron, and zinc. Amongst its favorable functions, the stimulation of the digestive processes stands out.

I am brilliant

Cucumber rolls

For the casing: 7⅔ cups (800 g) long cucumbers • **For the filling:** 1⅔ cup (250 g) avocado • ¾ cup (110 g) red pepper • ⅖ cup (75 g) yellow pepper • 1½ cups (200 g) shitake • **Condiments to marinade the shitake:** less than 1 tablespoon (1 g) fresh cilantro • less than 1 teaspoon (3 g) fresh ginger • 3 teaspoons (8 g) garlic • 5 teaspoons (25 ml) lemon juice • 2 teaspoons (10 ml) agave • 4 tablespoons (55 ml) olive oil • salt

To prepare the casing:

1 Peel the cucumbers and cut them in to very fine slices, with the help of a mandolin.

2 Place the layers of cucumber in a way to form a square. Repeat the process until the slices are done.

To prepare the filling:

1 Wash the peppers, get rid of the seeds, and cut them, julienne style.

2 Peel, remove the pip from, and cut the avocado into strips.

3 Prepare the shitake.

To prepare the shitake:

1 Clean and separate the heads of the mushrooms and cut them into strips.

2 Peel the garlic and grate it.

3 Grate the ginger.

4 Chop the cilantro.

5 Place the ginger and cilantro on a tray. Add the olive oil, lemon juice, agave, and salt. Mix well and then add the shitake mushrooms. Mix gently and let it marinade for 1 hour.

6 Before using the mushrooms, drain them.

Assembling the rolls:

1 In each one of the squares formed by the cucumber slices, add a small portion of peppers, the shitake marinade, and the avocadoes.

2 Wrap like a roll.

Let yourself be swept up by the energy of this bite.

Cilantro

This plant also goes by the name "Chinese parsley." Its potent flavor and strong aroma are fundamental in the kitchen of that country and also in South America. The seeds are used as a spice, powdered or whole, while the leaves, whose taste are most distinct, are used as aromatic herbs. Either can be added to a multitude of plates, to those that contribute to their carminative properties.

I am a game
Zucchini cannelloni

Its flavor will surprise you so much that you will want to share it.

For the casing: 3 cups (380 g) zucchini • salt • **For the filling:** 1 teaspoon (3 g) hiziki seaweed • 6 tablespoons (20 g) dehydrated tomatoes • 2 cups (250 g) carrots • ½ cup (80g) soft onion • 2 teaspoons (10 ml) walnut oil • a pinch of nutmeg • ⅛ cup (20 g) walnuts • ¼ teaspoon (.5 g) ground sage • green sunflower sprouts • **For the almond cream:** ½ cup (75 g) raw almonds • 5 tablespoons (75 ml) water • **For the sauce:** ½ cup (70 g) red pepper • ⅔ cup (100 g) tomato • 1 teaspoon (3 g) garlic • 2 teaspoons (10 ml) olive oil • less than ⅛ cup (9 g) walnuts • turmeric • aromatic salt

To prepare the casing:

1 Peel the zucchini and cut it lengthwise in very fine slices.

2 Lay out the slices on a flat tray and salt them lightly so that part of the water gets removed.

To prepare the filling:

1 Soak the hiziki for 2 hours and drain.

2 Soak the walnuts for 2 hours. Drain them and shred them or chop them with a knife.

3 Soak the dehydrated tomatoes at least 1 hour and drain them. Then cut them into pieces.

4 Peel and cut the carrots into very fine pieces.

5 Peel and cut the onion julienne style.

6 On a tray, mix all the ingredients for the filling except the hiziki and the green sprouts, and let it rest at least 30 minutes.

To prepare the almond cream:
See recipe *I am laughter*, p. 160.

To prepare the sauce:

1 Soak the walnuts 6 hours and then, drain them.

2 Wash, extract the seeds from, and cut the red pepper.

3 Peel the garlic.

4 Peel and remove the pips from the tomato.

5 Blend the ingredients until you get a fine sauce.

Assembling the cannelloni:

1 Place on a plate 5 layered slices of zucchini.

2 Put the filling on top and add a small amount of hiziki, almond cream, and the green sunflower sprouts.

3 Roll up and repeat the process until you're out of ingredients.

4 Accompany the dish with the sauce.

❉　❉　❉　❉

Note: The zucchini cannelloni can be served as such or cut as if they were sushi.

I am intelligence

Zucchini noodles

3 pounds (1¼ kg) zucchini • salt

1 Peel the zucchini and cut them into strips in the shape of noodles (with a machine that makes vegetable noodles). Another option is to grate them in the shape you desire.

2 Put them in a colander, salt them, and let them sit a minimum of 30 minutes. The salt helps the zucchini lose water and break its rigid structure. If a drier texture is desired, they can be dried with a cloth or paper towel.

3 Now they are ready to be served accompanied by whatever sauce, condiment, or vegetables.

Note: These noodles are delicious with a mustard vinaigrette or tomato vinaigrette sauce.

Zucchini

Vegetable used in a varied range of gastronomic preparations, which have a great proportion of water and less caloric content. It is composed of the following: carbohydrates, potassium, magnesium, phosphorus, pholates, and small amounts of vitamin C. It is easy to digest and has a mild laxative effect.

I am exuberant

Stuffed tomatoes

4¾ cups (760 g) tomatoes • dry garlic powder • **For the stuffing:** 2 cups (300 g) yellow pepper • 1 cup (150 g) green pepper • ¾ cup leek (white part) • 1 teaspoon (3 g) garlic • 2 teaspoons (10 ml) olive oil • ³⁄₁₀ teaspoon (2 g) salt • less than 1 teaspoon (1 g) curry powder

1 Peel the tomatoes, cut them in half, and take out the pips.

2 Season it with the dry garlic powder.

3 Put them in the dehydrator until they show a softer texture.

4 When the tomatoes are ready, stuff them with the vegetable mixture.

To prepare the stuffing:

1 Wash the peppers and set aside the seeds. Cut them into very tiny pieces.

2 Chop the leeks very finely.

3 Peel and chop the garlic.

4 Place the cut-up veggies in a big bowl and mix them with the salt, olive oil, garlic, and curry powder.

5 Dehydrate this preparation until you get a softer texture.

Note: They can be served with crackers.

Vibrant color; fragrant aroma.

Leek

Related to the onion and garlic. We can find it all year round. Nevertheless, it is strongest and has a more accentuated flavor during the cold months. It provides a notable amount of fiber, potassium (an ally of good renal functions), and vitamins (folic acid, B1, C, and E) to the dishes. It is also rich in flavonoids (antioxidants) and sulphurous compounds. Those sulphurous compounds are found in lesser proportion than in garlic and onion, and are responsible for their peculiar odor and taste. Concerning its virtues, its positive effects on respiratory illnesses, particularly those that affect the bronchial tubes, are known. In addition it is depurative and a diuretic.

I am spring
Zucchini filled with spinach

4½ cups (550 g) small zucchini • Parmesan cheese (see recipe **I am patience**, p. 161) • salt • **For the stuffing:** 2⅔ cups (80 g) spinach • ⅓ cup (50 g) pine nuts • ¼ cup (40 g) red or yellow pepper • ⅕ cup cup (30 g) onion • 1 clove garlic • less than 1 tablespoon (1.5 g) parsley • pepper • salt

1 Peel and cut the zucchini through the middle. Hollow them out, salt them, and let them sit for 2 hours.

2 Once this time has passed, get rid of any water present, and fill them.

3 In the moment of serving, add Parmesan cheese on top.

To prepare the stuffing:

1 Soak the pine nuts a minimum of 2 hours and drain them.

2 Wash the spinach and drain it.

3 In the food processor, blend the surplus zucchini, together with the pine nuts and spinach, careful not to lose water.

4 Wash the red or yellow pepper, get rid of the seeds, and cut the pepper in tiny pieces.

5 Peel the onion and garlic and chop them into small pieces.

6 Chop the parsley and, on a tray, mix it with the peppers, garlic, and onion with the blended zucchini, pine nuts, and spinach. Add salt and pepper.

Option: Before adding the Parmesan cheese, the stuffed zucchini can be dehydrated for about 2 hours. Thus it will obtain a softer texture.

Fly with them; your destination, the springtime.

Spinach
A vegetable that's rich in protein, provitamin A, vitamin C, folic acid, magnesium, iron, calcium, and diverse essential nutrients. Its portion of lutein and zeaxanthin has retina-protecting and retina-defending effects. And the carotenoids, with their antioxidant effects, prevent the loss of the visual acumen.

I am a flower

Garbanzo bean sprouts

1⅔ cups (125 g) garbanzo bean sprouts • 1 cup (150 g) red pepper • 1½ cup (120 g) champignon mushrooms • 3 tablespoons (40 ml) tamari • 4 teaspoons (20 ml) olive oil • **For the salsa:** 5 raw almonds • 5 raw hazelnuts • less than 1 teaspoon (3 g) ñora peppers • sprinkle (.3) of red pepper • less than 1 teaspoon (1 g) garlic • 5 teaspoons (6 g) dehydrated tomatoes • 2 tablespoons (30 ml) olive oil • 3 tablespoons (45 ml) water • salt • pepper

1 Clean and cut the champignon mushrooms into small pieces and put them on a tray to marinade with olive oil and tamari for an hour.

2 Wash and cut the red pepper without seeds into small squares.

3 Mix the marinated and drained mushrooms together with the garbanzo bean sprouts, the cut up pepper, and the sauce. Let it marinade.

To prepare the sauce:

1 Peel the garlic and cut and remove the pips from the ñora peppers.

2 With the help of a blender, blend all the sauce ingredients at once.

Note: To germinate your own garbanzos, see the chapter on sprouting.

A full dish of sprouted life.

Pepper

It is one of the hot-flavored spices with an intense aroma that is most popular and most used nowadays. Even when it is used in moderation, it is capable of changing the flavor of the dishes in an amazing way. It is advised to keep it as grains while storing and to grind it the moment you are using it. It stands out for its ability to stimulate the production of digestive juices, facilitating these kinds of processes, and contributing to the reduction of the intestinal gases.

I am passion

Grilled vegetables

1 cup (250 ml) of pineapple juice • 2 tablespoons (30 ml) olive oil • 2 tablespoons (25 ml) agave • 2 teaspoons (13 g) salt • 4 tablespoons (12 g) garlic • 3½ cups (500 g) onion • 4 cups (600 g) pepper (just red, or red and green)

1 Peel and chop the garlic. Place it together with the pineapple juice, 4 teaspoons (20 ml) of olive oil, agave, and a sprinkle (10 g) of salt. Mix it all.

2 Peel the onions and cut them into boats a half a finger in thickness.

3 Add the onions to the liquid preparation and let them marinade for a whole night.

4 The next day, wash and dry the seeds of the peppers, cut them julienne style, and add to them 2 teaspoons (10 ml) of olive oil and ½ teaspoon (3 g) of salt.

5 Let the pepper and the onion, drained from the marinade, dehydrate separately. Dehydrate until they have obtained the texture of grilled vegetables, for 4-5 hours.

Note: This dish can be served accompanied by whatever sauce (pesto, romesco, vinaigrette . . .) and/ or other fresh vegetables. With the excess marinade, a delicious sauce can be made (see recipe **I am tranquility**, p. 156).

Garlic

Its strong flavor and aroma, intensely unique, make it an essential condiment that is used in many different ways: whole, grated, chopped, as a powder, and blended; preferably, as recommended in the diverse culinary preparations, like sauces, marinades, etc. Because of the sulphurous compounds that it contains, many of the beneficial medicinal properties are known: antibiotic, diuretic, vasodilator, and depurative, amongst others.

I am the sun

Cauliflower "couscous"

3 cups (300 g) cauliflower • 1 tablespoon (15 g) sesame seeds • 2 teaspoons (2 g) turmeric • less than 1 teaspoon (2.5 g) salt • 4 teaspoons (20 ml) lemon juice • 4 teaspoons (20 ml) olive oil

1 In a food processor, blend the cauliflower (without the green leaves) until you've obtained a texture similar to that of couscous.

2 Place it in a bowl, together with the ground sesame seeds, tumeric, lemon juice, olive oil, and salt. Mix the ingredients softly.

3 For the presentation, and with the help of a cup, make medium balls with the aforementioned mixture and place them on the plate. You can use vegetables or marinated mushrooms as a side.

Note: We use the name "couscous" because with the cauliflower prepared as such a similar texture is obtained. You can also substitute the sesame seed for ³⁄₁₀ cup (8 g) parsley.

With each bite we move to the soft desert sand, heated by the sun.

Tumeric

Tumeric is a spice originating from India. It has a bitter, lightly spicy flavor, with a trace of musk, which evokes orange and ginger. It is a popular condiment that is a part of the preparation of curry.

I am sensational

Vegetable timbale

For the cauliflower: 3 cups (300 g) cauliflower • 1 teaspoon (6 g) curry powder • 2 teaspoons (10 ml) olive oil • **For the cucumber:** 9½ cups (1 kg) cucumber • 1 tablespoon (12 g) fresh mint • ½ teaspoonful salt • ½ cup (70 g) soft onion • **For the tomato:** 2½ cups (400 g) tomato • 3 tablespoons (10 g) fresh oregano • a pinch of salt • **To decorate:** 1 large avocado

To prepare the cucumber:

1 Peel the cucumbers, grate them, and salt them. Put them in a drainer so the water drains.

2 Peel the onion.

3 Once the cucumbers are drained, mix them with the chopped mint and the soft, finely cut onion. Set it aside.

To prepare the tomatoes:

1 Peel and remove the pips from the tomatoes and cut them into small dice.

2 Mix them with the fresh oregano, chopped finely, and set aside.

Its presentation is a spectacle for our senses.

To prepare the cauliflower:

1 Blend the cauliflower (Without the green leaves) in a food processor until it is a texture similar to that of couscous.

2 Place it in a bowl and add the curry and olive oil. Mix.

To pile the vegetable timbale:

1 Use a mold that doesn't have a bottom and in its interior place the cauliflower, squeezing a little so that it stays lightly compact.

2 Above this first layer, add the cucumber. Afterward, arrange the tomatoes with a pinch of salt. To finish it up, take off the mold and decorate with a quarter of a peeled avocado, cut in the shape of a fan, above the tomato.

Curry

It is used, since the old days, in Indian cooking to make the dishes. It consists of a mix of spices, finely ground, combined according to the preferences of each chef. Sauces and dishes with very characteristic flavor and aroma can be prepared with the curry.

I am liberty

Spicy "rice"

For the "rice": 2½ cups (250 g) cauliflower • ½ cup (50 g) pine nuts • **Condiments for the marinade:** ½ cup (100 ml) olive oil • 2 cups (450 ml) orange juice • ½ teaspoon (3 g) salt • 2 teaspoon (6 g) garlic • ⅛ cup (18 g) onion • ⅛ cup (5 g) parsley • a pinch of cumin • salt • chili pepper • **Vegetables** ⅔ cup (60 g) broccoli • ⅔ cup (100 g) red pepper • ⅔ cup (100 g) sweet, soft, raw corn • ½ cup (50 g) carrots • 1 cup (150 g) tomatoes

To prepare the "rice":

1 Soak the pine nuts for about 2 hours. Once this time has passed, drain them.

2 In a food processor, blend the cauliflower (without the green leaves) together with the pine nuts, until obtaining a texture similar to rice.

To prepare the condiments for the marinade:

1 Peel the garlic and onion.

2 Place all the ingredients in the blender vessel and blend.

3 Once blended, put them in a bowl and let it sit until you have the vegetables cut.

To prepare the vegetables:

1 Separate the broccoli in small flowers.

2 Peel the carrots and cut them julienne style.

3 Wash, get rid of the seeds, and cut the red pepper into very fine strips.

4 Peel, remove the pips from the tomatoes, and cut them into strips.

5 Add the condiments to the bowl to marinate the broccoli, carrots, pepper, corn, and tomatoes. Let it rest for a minimum of about 2 hours so that the vegetables are soaked in flavor.

6 Once this time has passed, drain them.

To make the mound on the dish:
Place a base of rice and scatter the marinated vegetables on top.

Note: We use the name "rice" because with the cauliflower blended in this way, you get a similar texture. We can use the excess liquid from the marinade as a salad dressing.

In tasting this dish, we experience the flavor of Mexico.

I am a surprise

"Rice" with mushrooms

For the "rice": 2½ cups (250 g) cauliflower • 6 cups (50 g) of pine nuts • **To marinate the mushrooms:** 1¾ cups (150 g) Scotch bonnet mushrooms • 4 cloves (35 g) of garlic • 2 tablespoons (30 ml) olive oil • ⅓ cup (7 g) fresh basil • salt

To prepare the "rice":

1 Soak the pine nuts for 2 hours and drain them.

2 In a food processor, blend the cauliflower (without the green leaves) and the pine nuts until obtaining a texture similar to that of rice.

To prepare the mushrooms:

1 Peel and cut the garlic into small pieces.

2 Clean the mushrooms.

3 Chop the basil very small.

4 In a bowl, place the olive oil and salt. Continue to add the garlic, basil, and mushrooms, and stir with caution. Let it marinate for an hour minimum.

For presentation:

Mix the mushrooms with the "rice" using extreme caution and place it on the dish with a mold.

Note: This "rice" stays very well if we marinade the mushrooms with 1½ tablespoons (20 ml) of tamari instead of salt. We use the name "rice" because with the cauliflower blended in this form it obtains a similar texture.

A dish whose scent transports us to the heart of the forest.

I am growth

Pumpkin lasagna

1¾ cups (200 g) pumpkin • 1½ cup (150 g) soft shitake mushrooms • ⅔ cup (100 g) onion • 6 cups (200 g) spinach • 4 tablespoons (60 ml) olive oil • 2 teaspoons (10 ml) lemon juice • (1 g) of thyme • 4 cloves (12 g) garlic • 1 teaspoon (.5 g) sage powder • a pinch of black pepper • 1 tablespoon (15 ml) tamari • ⅖ cup (50 g) pine nuts • 1 teaspoon (1 g) fresh oregano • a few drops of stevia • salt

1 Peel the garlic and chop it finely.

2 Place it on a tray and add 2 teaspoons (10 ml) olive oil, 2 teaspoons (10 ml) of lemon juice, thyme, and sage powder. Stir to homogenize the ingredients.

3 Peel and cut the pumpkin finely, through the wider part, so that you have large slices.

4 Spread them out on a flat tray and add the garlic preparation on top of each of the slices. Let it marinade for approximately 1 hour (if you want the pumpkin slices to be softer, let them marinate for longer). To avoid making them curve while still maintaining their firmness, cover them with a piece of wax paper and put a weight on top.

5 Peel and cut the onion in fine slices, add salt and stevia, and mix so that the onion loses the water.

6 Clean and cut the shitake mushroom into pieces. On a tray, mix it with 3 tablespoons (40 ml) of olive oil, 3 teaspoons (15 ml) of tamari, oregano, and a pinch of black pepper. Let it rest for approximately 1 hour.

7 Soak the pine nuts for 2 hours and drain them.

8 Wash and drain the spinach very well. Place them in a food processor together with the pine nuts, 2 teaspoons (10 ml) of olive oil, and salt, and blend until the mixture is fine but not dry. Process it with caution, so that it doesn't pass the desired point, as the mixture will get rid of all the water.

9 Finally, arrange the ingredients in layers in the following order:

- 1 slice of pumpkin
- Spinach preparation
- 1 slice of pumpkin
- Shitake mushroom
- 1 slice of pumpkin
- Onion
- 1 slice of pumpkin

The pumpkin is a winter vegetable that inspires creativity.

I am splendor

Vegetable lasagna

4 cups (500 g) of zucchini • 6 cups (200 g) of spinach • 1 avocado • 1 cup (100 g) of fresh shitake mushrooms • 2⅓ cups (360 g) of mature tomatoes • 4 tablespoon (60 ml) of olive oil • 1 teaspoon (5 ml) of tamari • ⅓ cup (7 g) of fresh basil • salt • pepper

1 Cut the mushrooms into fine slices and marinate them with 4 spoonfuls of olive oil and tamari for 1 hour.

2 Peel the tomatoes, remove the pips, cut them into pieces, and marinate with 2 additional spoonfuls of olive oil and the finely chopped basil.

3 Peel and cut the zucchini in fine slices using the mandolin. Salt them lightly and let them release the water, for a minimum of ½ hour.

4 Wash and drain the spinach.

5 Peel and remove the pit from the avocado.

6 In a blender, continue to blend the spinach and avocado together, careful not to let the water out.

7 Finally, pile on the lasagna. For that process, place the ingredients according to this order:

- As a base, layers of zucchini.
- After, arrange the blended spinach.
- Continue with a layer of the marinated shitake mushroom.
- Place another layer of zucchini.
- Finally, add strips of tomatoes, and season with salt and pepper.

It provides harmony to the body and mind.

I am harmony

Zucchini Carpaccio pizza with dehydrated tomato, arugula, macadamia nut cheese, and pesto

A rainbow of colors.

For the base: 5 cups (630 g) of zucchini • salt • **For the toppings:** ¾ cup (15 g) of arugula • 1 cup (65 g) of dehydrated tomatoes • ¼ cup (46 g) of black olives • **For the fresh cheese:** ½ cup (70 g) of macadamia nuts • 2 tablespoon (35 ml) of water • salt • **For the pesto:** 3 tablespoon (40 ml) of olive oil • 1 tablespoon (10 g) of pine nuts • ½ cup (8 g) of fresh basil • less than 1 teaspoon (½ g) of fresh oregano • less than 1 teaspoon (1⅓ g) of garlic • salt

To prepare the base:
Wash and slice the zucchini. Salt it and let it sit a minimum of 30 minutes so that the water is released.

To prepare the toppings:
1 Soak the dehydrated tomatoes a minimum of 1 hour, until they are soft. After, drain them and cut them into small pieces.

2 Remove the pits from the olives and chop them.

3 Wash and drain the arugula.

To prepare the fresh cheese:
1 Soak the macadamia nuts for about 2 hours. Once this time has passed, drain them.

2 Put the macadamia nuts, the salt, and water in the blender vessel, and blend until you have a preparation with a thick texture, similar to that of fresh cheese.

For the pesto:
1 Peel the garlic.

2 Mince the pine nuts, basil, oregano, garlic, and salt.

3 Continue to add the olive oil and stir well.

How to pile everything on the Carpaccio pizza:
1 First, prepare the base of the pizza only with the slices of zucchini. To do so, place them on a plate, overlapping, so they form circles. If you want, you can dry them a little with a cloth or paper towel.

2 Continue to add the tomatoes and olives, on top, as if it were a conventional pizza, and place the rucula in the middle of the Carpaccio pizza.

3 Finally, add 1 teaspoonful of cheese to distinct spots on the pizza and season with the pesto.

I am present

Cauliflower with shitake mushrooms

4½ cups (300 g) of cauliflower • ⅔ cup (100 g) of sweet, soft, raw corn • 2¼ cups (225 g) of shitake mushrooms • ¼ cup (7 g) of fresh basil • 2 teaspoons (2 g) of fresh oregano • 3 tablespoons (50 ml) of olive oil • 6 teaspoons (3 g) of fresh sage • 2 teaspoons (5 g) of garlic • 4 tablespoons (20 ml) of tamari • pepper • salt

1 Chop the basil, oregano, and sage into fine pieces, and put it all in a bowl.

2 Add the olive oil and tamari to the bowl with the aromatic herbs.

3 Peel and layer the garlic and add it to the mix.

4 Clean and cut the shitake mushroom into layers, add them to the preparation, and let it marinade for 1 hour.

5 Once this time has passed, separate the cauliflower into flowers and crumble the corn. Add everything to the bowl, with the aforementioned preparation, and continue to marinate, this time for 6-8 hours in the refrigerator.

6 Before serving, add salt and pepper.

Note: The smaller the flowers of cauliflower that are prepared in this recipe, the better.

Silent appearance for its simplicity.

Corn

A grain that is known and appreciated, for many eras, for its nutritious qualities. It contains an important proportion of carbohydrates and fiber, in addition to group B vitamins and beta-carotenes, which have an antioxidant effect.

I am a star

Quinoa croquettes

1 cup (140 g) of raw almonds • ½ cup (60 g) of pine nuts • ½ cup (95 g) of quinoa germinated for a day • 2 cups (170 g) of Chanterelle • 1 tablespoon (10 ml) of tamari • 4 teaspoon (20 ml) of olive oil • ½ cup (45 g) of celery • ³⁄₁₀ cups (45 g) of onion • ⅔ cup (95 g) of peeled tomato, without seeds • ½ cup (50 g) of cauliflower • (1 g) of fresh thyme • 1 teaspoon (1.5 g) of fresh oregano • 2 teaspoon (7 g) of garlic • 2 teaspoons (10 ml) of lime juice • ⅘ cups (100 g) of carrot • ⅙ cup (10 g) of parsley • salt

1 Soak the almonds between 24 and 48 hours. Every 12 hours change the water, rinsing beforehand. Once the soaking time has passed, drain them and peel them.

2 Soak the pine nuts for 2 hours. After, drain them.

3 Clean and cut the small mushrooms and, on a tray, let them marinate for 1 hour with the tamari and olive oil.

4 Peel and cut the onion, garlic, and carrot.

5 Wash the garlic, set aside the green leaves of the cauliflower, and cut the cauliflower into big pieces.

6 Place all the ingredients in the food processor and blend until you have a homogenous mix.

7 Finally, prepare the croquettes and place them on a sheet of teflex on top of the dehydrator tray. Dehydrate for about 10 hours, turning them over and putting them on for a couple of hours more to dehydrate without the teflex sheet.

Note: These croquettes can be eaten just after preparation or in any stage of the dehydration process. But, so it looks like a croquette, it is better to complete the process of dehydration.

Soft on the inside, crunchy on the outside.

Ingredients

For the base: 2 tablespoons (25 g) sunflower seed flour • ⅕ cup (25 g) buckwheat flour • ⅜ cup (50 g) walnuts • ⅓ cup (18 g) sun-dried tomatoes • 1⅗ cups (200 g) peeled apple • 3 teaspoons (8 g) garlic • sprinkle (¾ g) of dry basil • (5 ml) walnut oil • 1 teaspoon (¾ g) dry oregano • salt • **For the tomato sauce:** 1 ½ tablespoons (5 g) sun-dried tomatoes • ⅓ cup (55 g) fresh tomato • ⅖ cup (50 g) apple • less than 1 teaspoon (1 g) garlic • 2 teaspoons (10 ml) olive oil • 4 teaspoons (20 ml) water • sprinkle (⅖ g) dry basil • salt • **For the pesto:** 4 teaspoons (20 ml) olive oil • ⅕ cup (4 g) fresh basil • less than 1 teaspoon (2 g) garlic • 1/16 cup (3 g) parsley • 1½ tablespoons (12 g) pine nuts • 2 teaspoon (5 g) parmesan cheese made from pine nuts (see recipe *I am patience*, p. 161) • 1 tablespoon (20 ml) water • salt • **For the topping:** ⅜ cup (60 g) soft onion • ⅜ cup (70 g) red pepper • ½ cup (90 g) of broccoli • 1 ¾ cups (180 g) of shitake mushrooms • 4 tablespoons (60 ml) olive oil • 2 tablespoons (15 g) garlic • a pinch of rosemary • a pinch of thyme • 2 teaspoons (10 ml) tamari • 2¾ cups (450 g) tomatoes • salt

I am expansion

Vegetable pizza with pesto

To prepare the base:

1 Soak the walnuts for 6 hours and drain them.

2 Soak the dehydrated tomatoes for 1 hour and drain them.

3 Peel the garlic.

4 In a food processor, put the soaked tomato, garlic, apples, walnut oil, salt, walnuts, oregano, and dry basil. Blend everything well and add the sunflower pipes flour and the buckwheat flour, and return to mixing.

5 Spread out the dough over a sheet of teflex and place it on a dehydrator tray.

6 Dehydrate so it acquires the necessary consistency so you can turn it over. Then, remove the teflex sheet and place the dough directly on the tray. Continue dehydrating until it has a dry texture, but not rigid.

To prepare the tomato sauce:

1 Soak the dehydrated tomatoes for 1 hour and drain them.

2 Peel and cut the apple and garlic into big pieces.

3 Peel and remove the pips from the fresh tomato.

4 Place the apple, garlic, tomato, olive oil, water, basil, and salt in the blender vessel, and beat everything well until you get the sauce.

To prepare the pesto:

Peel the garlic and place it with all the ingredients in the blender vessel. Beat until you have a thick sauce.

To prepare the ingredients for the toppings:

1 Separate the trunk from the mushrooms. Clean and cut the heads into pieces and, on a tray, marinate in olive oil, tamari, peeled and chopped garlic, rosemary, and thyme for 2 hours.

2 Peel the onion and cut it julienne style. Wash and remove the seeds of the red pepper and cut it julienne style. Separate the broccoli flowers.

3 Peel and remove the pips from the tomatoes, and cut them into strips.

4 On another tray, mix all the ingredients with the shitake mushroom and pesto. Let it rest for about 30 minutes.

To "build" the pizza:

About 15 minutes before serving, prepare the pizza. Start by covering the base with tomato sauce and place the marinated vegetables on top. If you'd like, you can add small pieces of pine nut parmesan cheese, olives . . . It can be kept in the dehydrator just before serving.

Note: To prepare the sunflower pipes flour, soak the seeds for 6 hours. Afterward, drain them and dehydrate them until they are dry. Once dehydrated, blend them into flour. To make buckwheat flour, follow the same procedure but soak for only 30 minutes.

I am a breath

Tomato nigiri, shitake mushrooms, and basil

For the "rice": 3¾ cups (375 g) of cauliflower • ¾ cup (95 g) of pine nuts • 5 teaspoons (25 ml) of olive oil • salt • **For the toppings:** (80 g) of dehydrated tomato • 1¼ cups (120 g) of shitake • 3 tablespoons (45 ml) of olive oil • 4 teaspoons (20 ml) of tamari • 1 teaspoon (4 g) of garlic • 2 tablespoons (4 g) of fresh basil • salt

To prepare the "rice":

1 Soak the pine nuts for 2 hours. Then, drain them.

2 In a food processor, blend the cauliflower (without the green leaves) together with the pine nuts, olive oil, and salt, until you have a preparation with a texture similar to that of rice.

To prepare the toppings:

1 Soak the dehydrated tomato for a minimum of 1 hour and, afterward, drain it.

2 Get rid of the shitake trunks. Clean and cut the heads into pieces and put them on a tray with the tamari, olive oil, chopped and peeled garlic, basil, salt, and tomato. Let it marinate a minimum of 30 minutes.

To build the nigiri:

In this case, the best thing is to use a mold that is specifically for nigiri. With this mold you can prepare squares of "rice" where the ingredients are spread out on top.

Note: If desirable, you can season the cauliflower (the "rice") with aromatic herbs and spices, rice vinegar, and a sweet condiment.

To taste it is like enjoying an oriental perfume.

I am a fantasy

Beet, onion, and ginger nigiri

For the "rice": 3¾ cups (375 g) of cauliflower • ¾ cup (95 g) of pine nuts • 5 teaspoons (25 ml) of olive oil • salt • **For the topping:** 1¾ cups (240 g) of beet • ⅔ cup (100 g) of onion • 4 teaspoons (8 g) of ginger • 5 teaspoons (25 ml) of olive oil • 6 teaspoons (1⅕ g) of salt • a pinch of sage powder

To prepare the "rice":

1 Soak the pine nuts for 2 hours and drain them.

2 In a blender, blend the cauliflower (without the green leaves) together with the pine nuts, olive oil, and salt, until obtaining a texture similar to that of rice.

To prepare the toppings:

1 Peel the beets and grate them very finely.

2 Peel the onions and chop them into small pieces.

3 Grate the ginger and, on a tray, mix it with the beets, onion, olive oil, salt, and a pinch of sage. Let it marinate for a minimum of 30 minutes.

To build the nigiri:

In this case, it is best to use a mold specific to nigiri. With this mold, you can prepare squares of "rice" where the ingredients are placed on top.

Note: If desired, the cauliflower (the "rice") can be seasoned with aromatic herbs and spices, with rice vinegar and a sweet condiment.

Sage

This plant, considered highly beneficial, is very aromatic, with many possibilities of culinary use (preferably when it is fresh), either alone or combined with other ingredients. In terms of nutrients, we much emphasize: vitamins B and C, in addition to diverse essential oils responsible for an array of medicinal properties. Amongst them, we will mention the following properties: styptic, carminative, antidiabetic, anti-inflammatory, digestive, and many more.

I am cunning

Tempuras

For the tempuras: 1 cup (160 g) pine nuts • 6 tablespoons (55 g) cashews • 3 cups (170 g) carrots • 1¼ cups (155 g) zucchini • 1¼ cups (115 g) broccoli • 3 tablespoons (50 ml) lemon juice • less than 1 teaspoon (1 g) cayenne pepper • 2 teaspoons (2 g) fresh oregano • 1 tablespoon (2 g) fresh basil • less than 1 teaspoon (2 g) salt • 5 tablespoons (80 ml) of water • **For the sauce:** 4 teaspoons (20 ml) tamari • 1 tablespoon (15 ml) agave • 3 teaspoons (5 g) sesame seeds

To prepare the tempuras:

1 Soak the pine nuts and cashews for about 2 hours and, after, drain them.

2 In a blender, place the dry, drained fruits together with the lemon juice, cayenne pepper, oregano, basil, salt, and water, and blend until you've obtained a thick cream.

3 Peel and cut the carrots into strips.

4 Peel the zucchini and cut it into strips.

5 Separate the broccoli into flowers.

6 Mix the vegetables well with the cream and shape the tempuras.

7 Continue to place them on a tray of the dehydrator, atop a sheet of teflex, and dehydrate them for 6 hours.

8 Turn each of the tempuras over and dehydrate for 2 more hours, or until you've reached the desired texture.

To prepare the sauce:
On a tray, add all the ingredients and beat them with a fork.

Note: Each vegetable can be prepared separately. To do so, mix each one of them with the cream and dehydrate. Upon serving, mix them together.

Delicious dish to transport you via the Asian aromas and flavors. You won't be able to eat just one!

Cayenne pepper

It is a type of very small chili pepper that has an extremely spicy flavor. It is used in very small doses (generally powdered). Cayenne peppers have digestive, stimulant, and antiseptic properties.

I am knowledge

Catalan spinach maki sushi

2 leaves of nori seaweed • **For the "rice":** 4 cups (400 g) cauliflower • 1½ cup (200 g) pine nuts • 2 tablespoons (30 ml) olive oil • salt • **For the stuffing:** 3⅓ cups (100 g) spinach • 2½ tablespoons (24 g) pine nuts • 1 teaspoon (5 ml) olive oil • ⅛ cup (20 g) raisins • salt • 10 drops of sesame seed oil

To prepare the "rice":

1 Soak the pine nuts for 2 hours. Afterward, drain them.

2 In a blender, blend the cauliflower (without the green leaves) together with the pine nuts, olive oil, and salt, until you've obtained a preparation with a texture similar to that of rice.

To prepare the stuffing ingredients:

1 Wash and drain the spinach.

2 In a blender, blend the spinach with the pine nuts, olive oil, and salt, until it is rather small, but before all of the water has been removed.

3 Add the raisins and the sesame seed oil. Mix well.

To build the maki sushi:

1 Place the nori seaweed on a working surface.

2 Spread out the rice over the whole seaweed, except the extremities, so you can close it well.

3 On the other side, put in the ingredients from the stuffing and roll the preparation.

4 After, seal with a little bit of water, and let it sit for about 5 minutes.

5 Cut in various pieces.

Nori seaweed

We tend to find it in the form of flat leaves of a dark color, obtained by pressing and drying. It stands out, above all, for its rich protein content. In addition, it is a food that lacks saturated fats and that, instead, contains a high proportion of minerals: potassium, calcium, magnesium, iron, and iodine. Its portion of provitamin A (beta-carotene) also stands out. From these minerals derive several beneficial properties: it is remineralizing, it favors a lowering of cholestrol, and it contributes to the elimination of heavy metals, amongst many others.

I am confidence

Hummus

¼ cup (55 g) of chickpeas sprouted for 2 days • 1 cup (140 g) almonds or cashews • ³⁄₁₀ cup (50 g) sesame seeds • 2 teaspoons (7 g) garlic • 3 tablespoons (40 ml) lemon juice • ½ cup (120 ml) water • 3 teaspoons (15 ml) olive oil • salt • pepper

1 Soak the almonds between 24 and 48 hours. Every 12 hours change the water, rinsing beforehand. Once past the soaking time, drain and peel them. If you use cashews, soak them for 6 hours and drain them.

2 Blend together the chickpeas, almonds or cashews, sesame seeds, peeled garlic, salt, and pepper, and add the liquids, slowly, until obtaining a paste with a fine texture.

Note: A good idea is to serve the humus with crackers or vegetable crudités. The chickpeas need to be sprouted for 2 days, but no more because they'll become bitter. To sprout your own chickpeas, see the chapter on sprouting.

Almonds

It is a popular nut that is very appreciated and is used a lot in Mediterranean gastronomy. Of exquisite flavor, it is an ingredient that is adapted for all kinds of dishes. It contains a high proportion of healthy fats, vitamin E, and a notable amount of proteins and fiber. Amongst its minerals, calcium, in addition to potassium, magnesium, and phosphorus, stands out. Its vitamin B1 and B2 content is also remarkable. Apart from its culinary use, almonds are used in the preparation of some beauty products.

I am an explosion

Onion and Parmesan puffs

⅛ cup (25 g) linseed • 6 tablespoons (90 ml) water • ¾ cup (80 g) parmesan (see recipe **I am patience**, p. 161) • 1 teaspoons (5 ml) tamari • ½ tablespoon (7 ml) agave • ½ cup (100 g) of peeled apple • a pinch of Cayenne pepper • less than 1 teaspoon (2 g) peeled garlic • sprinkle (½ g) dry basil • 1 tablespoon (2.5 g) fresh rosemary • pinch (1 g) of salt • 1 cup (165 g) peeled onion

1 Soak the linseeds for 1 hour minimum with 3 tablespoons (45 ml) of water.

2 Once this time has passed, spread them out on a tray of the dehydrator, above a teflex sheet, and dehydrate for about 8 hours. Turn them over and dehydrate for 2 more hours, until they are dried well.

3 Convert the Parmesan and linseeds to flour and mix them.

4 Add the flours to a blender and blend with the rest of the ingredients except the remaining water. Add water very slowly until you have a soft dough. Depending on the amount of water from the apple, you can use more or less water.

5 Form fritters and dehydrate for a minimum of 4 hours, on top of a sheet of teflex, and dehydrate until you've obtained the desired texture. These puffs are delicious if they stay dry on the outside and lightly moist on the inside.

I am multicolored

Chips

1 If you use fruits, choose those that are most mature and sweet. Cut them into slices (for example: apple, pears, banana, mango . . .). In the case of vegetables, choose the freshest and cut them into slices, layered . . . in whatever shape you desire (for example: zucchini, parsnip, turnip, carrot . . .).

2 Next, dehydrate them and set them aside when they are dry. They remain magnificent and natural chips, which can be eaten as an appetizer and/or between meals. In the case of the sweet chips, they disappear in the hands of children.

Note: Choosing high-quality ingredients will have a positive effect on the result. The chips can be seasoned with herbs, spices, sweeteners, etc. to achieve a variety of flavors.

I am a stimulant

Cabbage Sauerkraut

5 cups (500 g) green cabbage • 5 cups (700 g) beets • 1¾ cups (230 g) turnip

1 Choose 2 or 3 exterior leaves of the cabbage and save them.

2 Cut and grate the cabbage, beets, and turnip very fine, or blend them in a blender.

3 Fill a glass jar to the top with vegetables.

4 Place the previously selected cabbage leaves on top, without the central nerve, and press on the preparation until no air remains. Afterward, cover.

5 Once the jar is well sealed, cover it with a cloth and let it sit at room temperature. If the vegetables are grated well, 5 days can be sufficient to obtain sauerkraut. Instead, if they have been cut thicker, they can require 10 to 12 days or, even, up to 3 weeks.

6 Once the fermentation has been finalized, open the jar and discard the cauliflower leaves that you have put on top. Afterward, extract the juice and then the sauerkraut.

Sauerkraut can be conserved for various weeks, in well-sealed jars kept in the refrigerator.

Note: To change the flavor of the sauerkraut, add some grated vegetables, such as carrots, green peppers, celery, cauliflower, or seaweed like hiziki, kombu, and dulse. Aromatic herbs or spices (grains) can also be added. In the marketplace, special pans exist to make sauerkraut.

I am ideal

Maki sushi with peppers, olives, and avocado

2 leaves of nori seaweed • **For the "rice":** 4 cups (400 g) cauliflower • 1½ cups (200 g) pine nuts • 2 tablespoons (30 ml) olive oil • salt • **For the stuffing:** ⅙ cup (30 g) red pepper • ⅛ cup (30 g) olives • ½ cup (80 g) avocado

To prepare the "rice":

1 Soak the pine nuts for a minimum of 2 hours and, afterward, drain them.

2 In a blender, blend the cauliflower (without the green leaves) together with the pine nuts, olive oil, and salt, until obtaining a preparation with a texture similar to that of rice.

To prepare the stuffing:

1 Wash and remove the seeds from the red pepper, and cut it julienne style.

2 Peel, remove the pit of the avocado, and cut it into strips.

3 Remove the pit and cut the olives into small pieces.

To pile the maki sushi:

1 Place the nori on a work surface.

2 Spread out the "rice" on all the seaweed, except on the outside, so you can close it well.

3 On the other side, put the stuffing ingredients and roll it up.

4 Next, seal with a little bit of water, and let it rest for 5 minutes.

5 Cut in many pieces.

Mix of Oriental and Mediterranean flavor.

I am a fantasy

I am a breath

I am knowledge

I am ideal

Sauces

"The secret is in the sauce" is a phrase used in many kitchens that, in the case of creative raw cooking, is very true. A sauce can make a dish delicious. Here we show you various sauces that present different methods and ideas that you can enjoy so you can make your own versions and new creations.

I am hope

Mustard sauce with Herbes de Provence

3 tablespoons (40 ml) olive oil • 1 tablespoon (15 ml) lemon or vinegar juice • less than a tablespoon (5 g) mustard powder • 2 teaspoons (10 ml) agave • ³⁄₁₀ teaspoon (2 g) salt • sprinkle (½ g) black pepper • sprinkle (1 g) of Herbes de Provence

Place all the ingredients in a bowl and beat them with a fork until you have a smooth sauce.

✳   ✳   ✳   ✳

Note: This sauce has an intense flavor. With only a small amount you can season zucchini noodles or your daily salads.

I am music

Vinaigrette sauce of Modena

3 tablespoons (50 ml) olive oil • ⅔ cup (100 ml) water • 2 teaspoons (10 ml) vinegar from Modena • less than 1 teaspoon (2 g) garlic

1 Peel the garlic.

2 Put all the ingredients in the blender vessel and blend.

It is worth the effort to try it on a simple rucula and tomato salad.

I am special

Pumpkin seed sauce

½ cup (75 g) pumpkin seeds (green) • ½ cup (70 g) apple • 1 teaspoon (3 g) garlic • less than 1 teaspoon (1½ g) curry powder • 1 tablespoon (15 ml) apple vinegar • ½ cup (100 ml) water

1 Soak the pumpkin seeds for 6 hours and drain.

2 Peel the apple and garlic.

3 Blend all the ingredients together.

❄   ❄   ❄   ❄

Note: The green seeds have a very nice flavor and texture.

I am communication

Tomato sauce

1 cup (50 g) dehydrated tomatoes • 2 tablespoons (30 ml) olive oil • 1 teaspoon (3 g) garlic • sprinkle (1 g) of dry basil • less than 1 teaspoon (½ g) black pepper • ½ teaspoon (3 g) of salt • ⅔ cup (120 g) fresh tomato • 1 teaspoon (5 ml) agave • 1 cup (250 ml) water • less than 1 teaspoon (½ g) of dry thyme • sprinkle (½ g) of onion powder

1 Peel the garlic.

2 Peel the fresh tomato and place it in the blender vessel together with the rest of the ingredients. Blend until the mixture acquires the texture of a sauce.

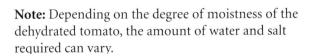

Note: Depending on the degree of moistness of the dehydrated tomato, the amount of water and salt required can vary.

I am expression

Pesto sauce

$7/10$ cup (160 ml) olive oil • ⅓ cup (40 g) pine nuts • 1½ cup (32 g) fresh basil • 2 teaspoons (2 g) fresh oregano • 2 teaspoons (5 g) garlic • salt

1 Peel the garlic.

2 In a food processor, mince the pine nuts, basil, salt, oregano, and garlic. It is important that the preparation isn't excessively smooth.

3 Next, add the olive oil and mix well.

❋ ❋ ❋ ❋

Note: It is very nice when you notice the distinct ground ingredients.

Basil

It is a plant with a pronounced and particular fragrance that can be used in a multitude of dishes, either in its fresh form, to better enjoy its intense aroma and flavor, or dried well. It is a main ingredient of the well-known pesto sauce. Amongst its virtues, we can emphasize: it is good for digestion, it increases blood circulation, it has an invigorating effect, it soothes, and it strengthens the nervous system.

I give thanks
Cashew mayonnaise

⅔ cup (120 g) cashews • 3 tablespoons (50 ml) olive oil • ½ cup (120 ml) water • salt

Soak the cashews for 6 hours. Drain them and blend them with the rest of the ingredients, until you have a sauce with a texture similar to that of mayonnaise.

Note: We can use our creativity and add our preferred ingredients. For example, before blending the sauce, garlic and/or tomato can be added to make a pink sauce, and/or red pepper with spices, or mint, or paprika and rosemary, etc.

I am tranquility

Pineapple and cashew sauce with onion fragrance

4 cups (650 g) pineapple • 4 teaspoons (20 ml) olive oil • 2 tablespoons (30 ml) agave • 1-2 teaspoons (10 g) salt • 4 teaspoons (12 g) garlic • 3 cups (500 g) onion • ½ cup (75 g) cashews • pepper

1 Prepare juice using the pineapple and pour it in a bowl.

2 Peel the garlic and chop it.

3 Add the olive oil, agave, salt, and chopped garlic to the pineapple juice, and mix it all well.

4 Peel the onions, cut them like boats half a finger in thickness, and add them to the liquid preparation. Let it macerate for a whole night.

5 The following day, get rid of the onion pieces from the marceration and place the liquid preparation in the blender vessel. Add the cashews and pepper, and blend.

Note: If you want this sauce to be thicker, you only have to vary the amount of cashews. The onion used can be dehydrated for about 4-5 hours until it has a texture like that of grilled vegetables.

I am tranquility

I give thanks

I am expression

Cheeses, Yogurts, and Crèmes

Cheeses, yogurts, and creams are authentic pleasures for the palate. They can be enjoyed alone or as individual ingredients in recipes. Here we show you some examples, but without a doubt many types exist that you can create and discover.

I am clarity

Almond yogurt

1 cup (150 g) raw almonds • ⅘ cup (200 g) rejuvelac

1 Soak the almonds for 48 hours. Every 12 hours change the water.

2 Once soaked, drain them and wash them.

3 Peel the almonds and blend them with the rejuvelac.

4 Once blended, put them in a bowl and cover it with a cloth. Let it sit 3-4 hours at room temperature so it ferments.

Note: This yogurt is delicious accompanied by honey or agave, cinnamon and/or fresh fruit.

Light, soft, harmonious . . .

I am laughter

Almond cream

1 cup (150 g) raw almonds • ⅗ cup (150 ml) water or rejuvelac

1 Soak the almonds for 48 hours. Every 12 hours change the water.

2 Once soaked, drain them and wash them.

3 Peel the almonds and blend them with the water or rejuvelac.

4 If it is made with rejuvelac, once blended, put them in a container, cover it with a cloth, and let it sit for 3-4 hours at room temperature so it ferments. If it is made with water, it can be used immediately once it is blended.

Note: This cream is ideal for adding to juices, soups, and salads. Made with water, it has a sweeter flavor, ideal for desserts. Agave, honey, or cinnamon can be added. With rejuvelac, it provides all the beneficial properties of water, but it has a more bitter flavor.

It will transport you to the country of your dreams.

I am patience

Parmesan cheese

1 cup (155 g) pine nuts • ⅓ cup (80 ml) rejuvelac • salt

1 Soak the pine nuts for 6 hours and drain them.

2 Blend the pine nuts together with the rejuvelac until you have a very smooth cream.

3 Put it in a bowl and cover with a cloth. Let it sit about 12 hours at room temperature so that it ferments.

4 Once past this time period, add salt, mix it with extreme caution, spread it on a sheet of teflex, and put it on a tray in the dehydrator. Dehydrate until it is well dried. Turn it over, cut it into pieces, and return to dehydrating until it is dried well.

Note: The flavor of this recipe is reminiscent of the typical Parmesan cheese. It can be used on salads, or in whatever other dish that appeals to us. It is convenient to keep it in a well-sealed container in a fresh, dry place.

It is slow to make, delicious to taste, and rich in its abundance of nutrients.

I am a dancer

Fresh cashew cheese with soft onion

⅘ cup (120 g) cashews • ⅔ cup (95 ml) rejuvelac • ⅛ cup (25 g) soft onion • 4 cloves (12 g) garlic • ½ cup (9 g) fresh basil

1 Soak the cashews for 6 hours and drain them.

2 Blend them with rejuvelac until you have a very smooth cream.

3 Put it in a bowl, cover it with a cloth, and let it sit for 12 hours at room temperature.

4 One this time has passed, add the onion and garlic to it, both peeled and cut very fine.

5 Also chop the basil and add it to the fresh cheese.

Note: It can be served immediately or let to rest so that the flavors mix. A fresh cheese can be enjoyed with bread, crackers, and salads. The recipe can be varied, by using capers with onion, for example, or a well dehydrated tomato with olives instead of soft onion, garlic, and basil.

A manna rained from the heavens.

I am clarity

I am patience

I am a dancer

Breads and Crackers

In this section we will discover that it is possible to enjoy delicious and aromatic breads and crackers, that have nice textures without even needing to bake. Whether they are sweet or salty, all of them are a gift for our body and senses.

I am serenity

Onion bread with olives

Enjoy this bread with tomato and let it surprise you . . .

½ cup (85 g) linseed • ¾ cup (90 g) walnuts • 1 cup (60 g) dehydrated onion • 1 tablespoon (14 g) garlic • 1¼ cups (160 g) peeled apple • ⅜ cup (80 g) green olives • 10 drops liquid stevia • 2 teaspoons (10 ml) olive oil • 1 cup (250 ml) water • salt

1 Soak the linseeds with 4/5 cup (190 ml) of water for 1 hour.

2 Spread them on a tray of the dehydrator over a sheet of teflex for about 8 hours. Turn them over and continue dehydrating a couple of hours more. When they are dried well, grind them until you have flour.

3 Soak the walnuts a minimum of 2 hours and drain them.

4 Peel and grate the garlic finely, and blend it with the walnuts, stevia, olive oil, salt, and 4 tablespoons (60 ml) of water.

5 Mix the linseed flour softly with the dehydrated onion cut into very small pieces.

6 Add to the aforementioned mix copped olives, finely grated apple, and the blend of walnuts, garlic, stevia, olive oil, salt, and water. Mix carefully and knead.

7 Once well kneaded, shape it like small rolls. If it is necessary, add more linseed flour to avoid the dough getting stuck to your hands (only for the exterior part).

8 On a tray of the dehydrator, place the rolls and dehydrate them until obtaining a dry texture on the outside and softer on the inside. Another alternative is to cut the rolls through the middle and to dehydrate them in two parts.

Note: Made in this way, the resulting bread will be soft on the inside and will have a light crunchy texture on the outside. It should be consumed in a couple of days, since even upon conserving the humidity, the product is altered by the passage of time. If we want to save it for longer we should dehydrate it completely until it is very dry. In this case, we recommend dehydrating it in parts. We can keep it in a well sealed container, in a dry and dark place, for several months.

To obtain a good dehydrated onion, you only have to peel the onion and cut it into fine slices to dehydrate them until they are dry enough. Save them in a hermetically sealed container in a dry and fresh place until they are needed.

I am beauty

Pumpkin seed crackers

1½ cups (200 g) pumpkin seeds (green) • ¾ cup (100 g) pine nuts • ⅞ cup (100 g) pumpkin • ¼ cup (45 g) soft onion • 5 tablespoons (30 g) celery • ½ cup (10 g) fresh basil • ¼ cup (6 g) parsley • 2 teaspoons (10 g) garlic • ¼ tablespoon (4 g) Chimichurri sauce • salt

1 Soak the pumpkin seeds and pine nuts for 6 hours. Afterward, drain.

2 Peel the garlic, soft onion, and pumpkin, and cut them into big pieces.

3 Wash and cut the garlic into pieces.

4 In a food processor, grind the pumpkin seeds and pine nuts, with the basil, Chimichurri, pumpkin, celery, onion, garlic, parsley, and salt, until it becomes a fine paste.

5 Spread it out over a teflex sheet on top of a dehydrator tray and dehydrate for about 10 hours. After turning it over, take out the teflex sheet and return to dehydrating for about 2 hours more, until they are dry and crunchy.

Pumpkin seeds

In addition to their nutritional richness, the consumption of pumpkin seeds is very interesting for their vermifuge properties (the capacity to eliminate intestinal parasites).

I am compassion

Carrot crackers

½ cup (65 g) sunflower seeds • ½ cup (85 g) linseed • 2⅓ cups (300 g) of carrots • 1 cup (110 g) celery • ⅓ cup (55 g) onion • 2-3 teaspoons (10 g) garlic • 2 teaspoons (2 g) oregano • less than 1 teaspoon (1.5 g) curry powder • 2 teaspoons (10 ml) olive oil • ⅘ cup (190 ml) water • salt

1 Soak the linseed a minimum of 1 hour in ¾ cup (190 ml) of water and the sunflower seeds a minimum of 2 hours in a lot of water.

2 Once this time has passed, drain the sunflower seeds and, in a food processor, blend them together with the linseed.

3 Peel and cut up the carrots and onion.

4 Cut the celery into pieces and peel the garlic.

5 Add the carrot, onion, celery, garlic, and the rest of the ingredients to the ground seeds. Blend until you have a fine texture.

6 Spread out the preparation on the whole surface of a sheet of teflex over a tray of the dehydrator.

7 Shape the crackers as desired, as squares, triangles, or rhombuses.

8 Next, dehydrate for 8 hours. Turn it over, taking out the teflex sheet. Let it dehydrate about 2 hours more or until they are crunchy.

Oregano

Plant with intense aroma that provides notable resources in culinary preparations, used as much in the fresh form as in the dried form. Like the majority of aromatic plants, it has medicinal properties due to their complex composition. Amongst them we can emphasize the following properties: antioxidant, anti-inflammatory, antimicrobial, sedative, antifungal, diueretic, anti-asthmatic . . .

I am serenity

I am compassion

I am curiosity

I am audacious

I am love

I am understanding

I am love

Tomato bread

2 cups (300 g) linseed • ¾ cup (100 g) walnuts • ⅘ cup (100 g) apple • 3 cups (700 ml) water • ¾ cup (40 g) dehydrated tomatoes • ¹⁄₁₀ cup (2 g) dry basil • 2 teaspoons (2 g) dry oregano • sprinkle (4 g) salt

1 Soak the linseed for 1 hour minimum with 2½ cups (590 ml) of water.

2 Afterward, spread them out on a dehydrator tray above a teflex sheet and dehydrate for 8 hours. Turn them over and return to dehydrating for 2 hours more until they are dried well. Then, grind them until you have flour.

3 Soak the walnuts a minimum of 2 hours and drain them.

4 Soak the dehydrated tomatoes for 1 hour. After, drain them.

5 Place the walnuts in the blender vessel and blend them with ⅖ cup (95 ml) of water and the tomatoes.

6 Peel the apple and grate them.

7 Put the linseed flour in a container, add the grated apple, the blended walnuts with the water and tomato, and the rest of the ingredients. Knead cautiously with your hands until obtaining a thick dough (the denser the dough is, the better the bread will be).

8 Give it the shape of a bread. Afterward, cut it into slices a finger in thickness as a maximum and place them in the dehydrator, until obtaining the desired consistency. Turn the slices over to get a uniform dryness.

✳   ✳   ✳   ✳

Note: It can be dehydrated so that it has a soft texture on the inside and a light crunch on the outside, but in this case it needs to be consumed in a couple of days maximum.

If it is left in the dehydrator for longer and it is totally desiccated, its texture will be similar to that of dry toast. In this case, it can be saved for several months in a well-sealed container, in a dry and dark place.

A surprising tomato bread.
Enjoy it with some olives, and you will see . . .

I am curiosity

Sweetened bread

⅔ cup (110 g) of linseed • ¾ cup (90 g) walnuts • 1½ cups (200 g) carrots • 1½ cups (200 g) apples • 1 teaspoon (4 g) of ginger • ⅓ cup (80 ml) honey • 1 cup (235 ml) water

1 Soak the linseeds for 1 hour minimum with 1 cup (235 ml) of water.

2 After, spread them on a dehydrator tray over a teflex sheet and dehydrate for about 8 hours. Turn them over and continue dehydrating for 2 hours more. When they are dried well, grind them until you have flour.

3 Soak the walnuts for a minimum of 2 hours.

4 Drain them, grind them in a food processor, and add them to the linseed flour. Knead with your hands.

5 Peel the carrots and apples, and grate them very finely.

6 Add them to the dough and mix softly.

7 Grate the ginger and incorporate it, together with the honey, into the dough. Work the preparation well, so all the ingredients are homogenized.

8 Mold the dough in the shape of bread and, once molded, slice it with a sharp, moist knife. The knife is moist so we avoid having the dough stick to the knife.

9 Spread out the portions of bread over a tray of the dehydrator (it doesn't need the teflex sheet because the dough is already consistent) and it dehydrates for about 10 hours. Turn all of the slices over and dehydrate them for 2 more hours.

✻   ✻   ✻   ✻

Note: Marmalade, honey, and chocolate—they are ideal on this type of bread. It will have a soft texture on the inside and a light crunch on the outside, but it should be consumed in a couple of days at most. To make it with a texture of dry toast, leave it in the dehydrator for longer, until it is dried well. In this case, it can be kept for several months in a well sealed container, in a dry and dark place.

Sweet and delicious . . . chew it softly.

I am understanding

Tomato crackers

⅓ cup (65 g) linseed • ½ cup (75 g) sunflower seeds • 3 cups (500 g) fresh tomato • 4 cloves (50 g) garlic • ½ cup (25 g) dehydrated tomato • sprinkle (½ g) of black pepper • less than 1 teaspoon (1 g) dry thyme • ½ cup (130 ml) water

1 Soak the linseeds for 1 hour minimum with ½ cup (130 ml) of water; soak the sunflower seeds for a minimum of 2 hours in lot of water.

2 Soak the dehydrated tomato for an hour.

3 On the other hand, peel and remove the pips from the fresh tomatoes and place them in a drainer so that they lose the water.

4 Peel and cut the garlic.

5 Once the soaking time has passed, drain the sunflower seeds and dehydrated tomato.

6 In a processor, blend all the ingredients together, until obtaining a homogenous paste.

7 Spread it out on top of a tray of the dehydrator, above a teflex sheet.

8 Shape the crackers as desired square, triangles, or rhombuses.

9 Next, dehydrate them for 8 hours.

10 Turn over the portions, extract the teflex sheet, and continue dehydrating for about 2 hours more or until they are crunchy.

Crack, crack . . . you will not be able to eat only one!

Thyme

Plant that provides its noteworthy aroma, to be used as a condiment with many beneficial qualities. It contains essential oils and diverse bioactive principles, as well as vitamins B1 and C. In addition to assisting in the conservation of the foods, it has numerous properties; amongst them, these stand out: stimulates the appetite and digestion, serves as an anti-parasite, anticatarrhal, antimicrobial, antiseptic, cicatrizant, anti-spasm, carminative, expectorant, soft astringent, and invigorant.

I am audacious

Crackers with fresh mushrooms

⅖ cup (75 g) linseeds • ½ cup (80 g) sunflower seeds • ⅔ cup (100 g) onion • 5 ounces (150 g) soft mushrooms • ½ teaspoon (2 g) of dry Herbes de Provence • 2 tablespoons (30 ml) olive oil • 4 teaspoons (20 ml) tamari • ⅔ cup (150 ml) water

1 Soak the linseeds 1 hour minimum with ⅝ cup (150 ml) of water and the sunflower seeds a minimum of 2 hours with abundant water.

2 Clean and cut the mushrooms in slices and put them in a container with the olive oil, tamari, and Herbs de Provence. Let it marinate for 1 hour.

3 Peel and cut the onion.

4 Drain the sunflower seeds and mushrooms, and put them in a food processor, together with the linseeds and onion. Blend until you have a paste.

5 Spread out the mix on top of a dehydrator tray, above a sheet of teflex.

6 Shape the crackers as desired (squares, triangles, rhombuses . . .), and dehydrate them for 8 hours.

7 Next, turn it over and extract the teflex sheet. Continue dehydrating for 2 hours more or until they are crunchy enough.

Crunchy, with the smell of the forest.

Sunflower seeds

These seeds form part of the inflorescence of the sunflower. It contains a notable amount of polyunsaturated fats, proteins, and fiber, in addition to vitamin E, vitamin B1 (thiamine), and B9 (folic acid). Its contribution of potassium, phosphorus, magnesium, calcium, and iron also stand out. From this arsenal, you get the following properties: cardiovascular protector and antioxidants to help brain functioning and for skin care.

Sweets

Healthy, juicy . . . we enjoy all those delicious sweet plates that surprise us. There seems to always be an option to help satisfy a tempting chocolate. But here there are options for all tastes, from the traditional fruit salad to a cake of the most exotic dried fruits. In addition, it is not necessary to spend a lot of time in the kitchen to prepare a delicious dish. The secret is in doing a good job choosing the ingredients and using your imagination a bit.

I am experience

Cream of chestnut

¾ cup (100 g) dry chestnuts • 5 tablespoons (50 g) macadamia or cashew nuts • 4 teaspoons (20 ml) agave
• ⅗ cup (150 ml) water

I Blend the dry chestnuts in a blender until you have flour. Repeat the same process with the macadamia or cashew nuts.

2 Put the two flours in the blender, add the water and agave, and blend all again until you have a cream.

3 Distribute it in individual cups and refrigerate.

✳   ✳   ✳   ✳

Note: Although it could be eaten just as so, ideally you want to let it rest for the sufficient amount of time so that the dry part of the flour totally absorbs the water that has been added. For example, if it is prepared around noon, ideally you would consume it at night or, even the next morning. Keep in mind that this cream cannot be saved more than 24 hours because it deteriorates.

Soft and sweet . . .and also filling.

Chestnuts

The appearance of the first chestnuts in the market marks the beginning of autumn. It is one of the nuts with the lowest amount of calories, on account of the fact that it has a low fat content (similar to grains and not to the rest of the nuts), and, instead, its water content is higher. In addition, it is rich in carbohydrates and fiber. There are numerous kinds of chestnuts distributed throughout the world.

I am a renovator

Diced apples and pineapple with cashew cream

2½ cups (300 g) of sweet apples • 1¾ cups (300 g) of fresh pineapple without the skin or core • **For the cream:** ⅓ cup (20 g) fresh coconut • ½ cup (65 g) cashews • 5 tablespoons (70 ml) agave • ⅖ cup (100 ml) of water • 1 teaspoonful of coffee of vanilla extract without alcohol • a pinch of salt

1 Peel and dice the apples into small pieces. Dice the pineapple in the same way.

2 Add the diced fruits to the cream and mix well so that the apples are not oxidized. Refrigerate for a minimum of 30 minutes.

To make the cream:

1 Soak the cashews for 6 hours and drain.

2 Place them in the blender vessel and add the rest of the ingredients for the cream. Blend it all together until it makes a very fine liquid, and place it in a bowl.

The success of such a simple dish serves as a surprise.

I am optimistic

Sweet pineapple

3⅔ cups (600 g) sweet pineapple • 2 cups (430 g) pears • 3 teaspoons (4 g) ginger root • 3 tablespoons (50 ml) pineapple juice • cocoa cream (optional: see recipe **I am divine**, p. 181)

1 Peel and cut the pears and pineapple into small cubes.

2 Put the fruit in a bowl together with the pineapple juice and mix well so that the pears don't oxidize.

3 Grate the ginger, add it to the fruits, and mix well.

4 Put the mixture into cups and, if you want, add a little cocoa cream.

Happily enjoy the view and let it elevate the spirit.

I am the light
Rolled almonds, dates, and apple

4¾ cups (600 g) of apple • 2 cups (280 g) raw almonds with skin • 1¼ cups (210 g) dates

1 Soak the almonds for 24 to 48 hours. Change the water every 12 hours. Once soaked, drain them, wash them, and then peel them.

2 Peel and cut the apples into very fine slices.

3 On a tray of the dehydrator, and over a sheet of teflex, place the apple slices partially overlapping one another, until they cover the whole surface. It is recommended to put a weight on top of them (for example, another tray), so that they stay flat while they dehydrate.

4 Dehydrate for 8 hours. Turn them over, remove the teflex sheet, and return to dehydrating for 8 more hours, maintaining the weight on top. It is important that they stay dry, but sufficiently soft to mold it.

5 Meanwhile, blend the almonds and dates (without pits) in a food processor, until you have a smooth dough.

6 Once the apple is dehydrated, cut it into squares approximately 2 inches x 2 inches (5 cm x 5 cm) in size.

7 Fill the apple squares with the aforementioned dough, and form little rolls, as if they were small cannelloni. Keep them in a fresh, dry place.

This sweet dish opens a light to our heart.

I am bondage

Small coconut and carrot pastry

1 cup (75 g) fresh coconut • 1 cup (130 g) carrots • ½ cup (80 g) of currants • 1 cup (130 g) zucchini • cinnamon to sprinkle

1 Peel the carrots and zucchini.

2 Mix in a food processor (i.e. Champion) the following: carrot, coconut, and pumpkin, until you've made a dough with a uniform texture, similar to that of wet flour.

3 Place the processed ingredients on a tray, add the currants without soaking, and mix it all in a homogenous form.

4 With the help of a bottomless mold, make small pastries out of the mix. It can also be done without the mold, in whatever shape you want.

5 Let it sit in the refrigerator for a minimum of 2 hours.

6 Upon serving, sprinkle with cinnamon.

Note: This dish, of exquisite sweet flavor, is ideally prepared with 12–24 hours in advance, due to the fact that the water should be evaporated partially to achieve a more intense flavor.

A perfect combination of ingredients that invites us to enjoy it on an autumn day.

I am subtle

Pineapple Carpaccio with strawberry tartar sauce

2½ cups (370 g) strawberries • 2 cup (300 g) pineapple • 3½ tablespoons (50 ml) agave • 2 teaspoons (10 ml) lemon juice • a pinch of salt

1 Wash the strawberries, get rid of the leaves, and cut them into very small squares.

2 Next, marinate the fruit with the agave, lemon juice, and a pinch of salt, for a minimum of 2 hours so they are mixed properly and absorb the flavors well. Once this time has passed, drain.

3 Peel the pineapple and cut it into very fine slices.

4 As a base, arrange the pineapple pieces covering the whole surface of the plate and place in the center of the strawberry marinade. Serve immediately.

Note: Be sure that the pineapple is sweet enough.

Fresh, smooth . . .perfect for a hot spring day.

I am divine

Cocoa cream

1⅖ cups (200 g) of cashews • ½ cup (55 g) of pure powdered cocoa • 8½ tablespoons (120 ml) of agave • ⅗ cup (100 ml) water

1 Grind the cashews into flour.

2 Place all the ingredients in the blender vessel and blend until you have a homogenous cream.

3 Let the mixture rest for 2–3 hours minimum. Thus, the flour will absorb the water and will obtain a truly uniform taste.

Note: It is an excellent cream with which to decorate sweet dishes like pastries, crepes, compotes, etc.

A feast of the gods enjoyed in small portions that enlivens the heart and spirit.

I am cordial

Cocoa mousse

3 cups (500 g) avocado • 1 cup (100 g) of cocoa
• 8 teaspoons (4 g) of dehydrated orange peel powder • 6
tablespoons (80 ml) of agave • ⅖ cup (100 ml) of water

1 Peel and remove the pit from the avocadoes.

2 Place all the ingredients in a food processor and
blend them until you've reached the desired
consistency.

*An authentic surprise
for our guests.*

3 Distribute the mousse in individual cups and keep
it in the refrigerator until you're ready to serve.

Note: In the case that carob powder is used (instead
of cocoa) it would only be necessary to use ½ cup
(55 g) of it.

I am a party

Cocoa crepes

1 cup (150 g) cashews • 8 tablespoons (165 g) agave
• ½ cup (45 g) powdered cocoa or ½ cup (55 g) of carob
• ⅖ cup (100 ml) water

1 Soak the cashews for 6 hours. Drain and
dehydrate them until they are dry enough.

2 Grind them into flour.

3 Add the rest of the ingredients and mix them
together.

4 On a dehydrator tray and on top of a teflex sheet,
shape the dough into crepes.

5 Dehydrate for 24 hours. Turn over, remove the
teflex sheet, and return to dehydrating for another
hour.

6 Fill with apple compote, cheeses, or whatever
you'd like.

I am a pleasure

Cocoa balls with orange coconut sauce

1 cup (150 g) cashews • ¼ cup (30 g) powdered cocoa • 1 teaspoon (⁷⁄₁₀ g) of dehydrated orange peel flour • ½ cup (50 g) grated coconut • 6 tablespoons (80 ml) agave

1 Soak the cashews for 6 hours. Drain them and dehydrate them until they are dry enough.

2 Grind them until you have flour.

3 Place the cashew flour, agave, cocoa, and orange peel flour in a food processor. Mix the ingredients well and let the dough sit in the refrigerator for 2 hours.

4 Once the time has passed, take out the dough from the refrigerator and work it, forming small marble shapes.

5 Roll around the cocoa balls in the grated coconut and let them sit in the refrigerator for another half hour.

Note: To obtain the orange peel flour, cut the orange peels (make sure they're previously washed), into fine strips and dehydrate. Once desiccated, continue grinding until obtaining the desired powder.

A party for our taste buds.

I am success

Pineapple marmalade

2¾ cups (460 g) pineapple without the skin • ⅓ cup (60 g) dehydrated pineapple • 3 tablespoons (45 ml) agave • 1½ teaspoon (5 g) of psyllium husk powder

1 Squeeze almost 2 cups (400 g) of pineapple to make pineapple juice. Set aside.

2 Chop ³⁄₁₀ cup (60 g) of remaining pineapple.

3 Chop the dehydrated pineapple into very small pieces.

4 Place the chopped natural pineapple, the dehydrated pineapple, the agave, and the psyllium husk powder into a bowl of juice. Mix it all very well and let it sit for 4 hours.

Note: A delicious recipe whether it's eaten alone or with sweet dishes, for breakfast, etc.

Psyllium
Refers to a rich supplement of nutritious fiber that comes from the seeds of diverse species of the Plantago genus (*Plantago ovata, Plantago isphagula, Plantago decumbens*). The parts that are used include the seed and the coat of the seed. Both are very rich in soluble fiber, which forms a viscous gel composed mainly of polysaccharides in the intestine. What results is an ideal nutritious complement that combats constipation.

I am beauty

Sweet crepes

They are divine eaten alone and spectacular when accompanied by fruits.

⅓ cup (50 g) macadamia nuts • 7 tablespoons (50 g) flaxseed meal • 2⅔ cups (200 g) apple • ⅘ cup (200 ml) water • 1½ tablespoon (20 ml) agave • a pinch of salt

1 Grind the macadamia nuts.

2 Peel and cut up the apple.

3 Blend all the ingredients in a food processor until you reach a fine, homogenous paste.

4 On a dehydrator tray, above a sheet of teflex, arrange the paste in the shape of crepes.

5 Dehydrate for 6 hours. Turn them over, remove the teflex sheet, and continue dehydrating for 2 more hours, until it has a texture of a dried, malleable crepe.

✳ ✳ ✳ ✳

Note: The best flaxseed meal is obtained by soaking the seeds in water, for at least an hour, dehydrating them until they're dry, and blending them until you have flaxseed meal.

I am unity

Fresh fruit ice cream

Natural fruit

1 Clean the fruit. Peel it (if necessary) and cut it into pieces. Save it in the freezer.

2 When it is frozen, put it through a Champion juicer, or a strong blender, until you have a creamy ice cream.

✳ ✳ ✳ ✳

Note: You can sweeten the ice cream upon serving. The banana, mango, strawberry, and pineapple flavors do a good job of staying fresh.

Your most natural ice cream.

I am peace

Apple compote

2¾ cups (350 g) apple • ⅕ cup (35 g) dehydrated apple • 1½ tablespoons (20 ml) agave • 2 teaspoons (10 ml) lime juice • a pinch of salt • cinnamon, to your liking

1 Peel the apples and cut them into pieces.

2 Place the pieces of apple together with the dehydrated apples, agave, lime juice, and pinch of salt in the vessel of the blender, and blend until you have a compote with a fine texture.

3 Upon serving, you can add cinnamon to your liking.

It's a certainty—you won't have ever tried such a delicious compote!

Agave

Agave syrup, also known as honey or agave nectar, is a sweet vegetable juice that is extracted from a plant of the name "blue agave" (*Tequilana webber*) in the form of transparent molasses and of a color that resembles clear honey. Its ability as a sweetener and delicious flavor make it an excellent culinary option.

I am celestial

Marinated apricot

6½ cups (1 kg) apricot • 3 tablespoons (40 ml) lemon juice • 7½ tablespoons (100 ml) agave • a pinch of salt

1 Wash and remove the pit from the apricots.

2 Place them in a bowl together with the lemon juice, salt, and agave.

3 Mix all the ingredients well and let them macerate for 3 hours. During this time, stir the mixture from time to time.

Note: Apricots can also be cut in small pieces, although if they are used in halves their appearance is spectacular. The juice that results from the maceration is an exquisite sweet shot without alcohol.

To enjoy this dish is like living in heaven.

I am knowledge

Marinated strawberries

2⅔ cups (400 g) strawberries • small drops of lemon • 15 drops liquid stevia • 2 teaspoons (10 ml) of agave

1 Wash the strawberries, remove the leaves, and cut them through the middle.

2 Add some drops of lemon, stevia, and agave, and stir with caution. Next, let macerate for half an hour.

An exquisite sweet for any celebration!

I am a celebration

Apple and strawberry pie

A dish full of flavor and festive color.

For the base: 1½ cups (200 g) raw almonds with shell • ⅜ cup (75 g) of dates • 4 teaspoons (20 ml) orange juice • 2 teaspoons (1 g) of dehydrated orange peel flour • **For the filling:** 8 cups (1⅖ kg) apple • 1½ cups (300 g) strawberries • (20 ml) agave • small drops of lemon juice • a pinch of salt • **For the marmalade:** 3 tablespoons (40 ml) agave • 1⅓ cups (200 g) strawberries • 5 drops of stevia • 1 teaspoon (3½ g) of psyllium husk powder

To make the base:

1 Soak the almonds for 48 hours. Change the water every 12 hours.

2 Once this time has passed, drain, wash, and peel them.

3 Place the almonds together with the dates (pitless), orange juice, and dried orange flour in a food processor, and blend until you have a thick, homogenous dough.

4 With this preparation, form a pie base and, afterward, dehydrate it until it stays dry.

For the filling:

1 Peel the apples, remove the core, make half-centimeter slices, and place on a dehydrator tray above a teflex sheet. Dehydrate until they have lost their moistness but are still soft.

2 Wash the strawberries, remove the leaves, and cut them down the middle.

3 Place them in a container and add 1 tablespoon (15 ml) of agave, some drops of lemon juice, and a pinch of salt. Let it marinate a half hour and drain.

For the marmalade:

Wash the strawberries and blend them with the psyllium powder, agave, and drops of stevia. Let it sit until you have a marmalade texture.

For the base:

Fill the base with the dehydrated apples. On top, place a fine layer of strawberry marmalade. Return to dehydrating so that it loses the moistness and, finally, is adorned on top with the strawberry halves.

I am imagination

Rolled apple and macadamia nuts

For the outside: ⅓ cup (50 g) macadamia nuts • 7 tablespoons (50 g) flaxseed powder • 1⅗ cups (200 g) apple • ⅘ cup (200 ml) water • 4 teaspoons (20 ml) agave • a pinch of salt • **For the filling:** 1 cup (160 g) of macadamia nuts • 2 teaspoons (10 ml) of lemon juice • 4 teaspoons (20 ml) of agave • 5 teaspoons (25 g) of cocoa butter • ⅘ cup (200 ml) water • 7⅕ cups (900 g) of apples

To prepare the outside:

1 Peel the apples and blend them with the rest of the ingredients until you have a fine cream.

2 Spread out on top of a teflex sheet, atop a dehydrator tray, all of the cream, in the shape of a square.

3 Dehydrate until it can be turned over. Upon doing that, remove the teflex sheet and continue dehydrating until you have a flexible roll.

To prepare the filling:

1 Peel and dice the apples. Dehydrate for about 6 hours, so that they are smooth but not dry.

2 Meanwhile, blend the macadamia nuts, lemon juice, agave, cocoa butter, and water until you have a homogenous cream.

3 Mix this preparation with the apples.

For the base:

1 Spread out the cream with the apples on top of the base, in a way that covers the whole surface, except two small sections at the ends.

2 Roll and let sit in the refrigerator for a couple of hours.

Note: To decorate you can use the recipe **I am divine**, p. 181, that you will see on top. The best flaxseed powder is obtained by soaking the seeds in water, for 1 hour minimum, dehydrating them until they are dry, and blending them until you have powder.

Creative, imaginative, and soft to the palate.

I am outstanding
Fig, raisin, and date bread

1⅓ cups (200 g) of dry figs • 2 cups (300 g) raisins • ⅞ cup (150 g) dates without the pit • ½ cup (50 g) almond flour

1 Blend all the ingredients in a food processor until you've obtained a homogenous paste.

2 Place the dough onto a plastic sheet and roll it.

3 Let it sit in the refrigerator for 1 hour.

4 Remove the plastic sheet.

5 After, slice it.

Note: If it is left to sit in the refrigerator, for about 8 hours, it is most delicious. To make the almond flour, soak the raw almonds for 24 to 48 hours, and every 12 hours change the water. Once soaked, drain, wash, peel, and dehydrate until they are dry. After, blend them to make flour.

A delicious sweet for all: the old and the young.

Dates
Dates, with a sweet and intense flavor, is one of the foods that concentrates its many nutrients in small doses. Its abundance of carbohydrates and fiber, which produces laxative properties, stands out.

I am fire

Crunch or granola

1 cup (130 g) hazelnut • 1 cup (130 g) pumpkin seeds • 1 cup (130 g) sunflower seeds • ¾ cup (100 g) sesame seeds • ¾ cup (50 g) coconut chips • ⅞ cup (130 g) of raisins without seeds • 1 cup (200 g) dates • 3½ tablespoons (50 ml) agave • 1⅓ cups (300 ml) orange juice

1 Soak the pumpkin, sunflower, sesame seeds, and hazelnuts for 6 hours.

2 Soak the raisins for 3 hours.

3 Once this time has passed, drain all of the soaked ingredients.

4 Remove the pits from the dates.

5 Make the orange juice, place it in the blender vessel together with the dates and agave, and blend.

6 Add the resulting blend to the rest of the ingredients and mix.

7 Scatter on a dehydrator tray with a teflex sheet or shape little granola bars. The dehydration time is long, for 2 days minimum. In the case of forming granola bars, remember to turn them occasionally.

Note: The bars are delicious at noon or midnight. We can use this crunch as breakfast, adding milk from nuts, apple, pear, etc.

Enjoy it, chewing slowly.

I am all heart

Baklava

⅓ cup (35 g) coconut balls • 6 tablespoons (80 ml) agave • ½ cup (75 g) cashews • 3 tablespoons (45 ml) orange juice • ⅛ cup (30 g) almond puree • 1 teaspoon (3 g) psyllium husk powder • 1–2 tablespoons (10 g) grated coconut

1 Beat the almond puree together with the psyllium powder and orange juice.

2 Grind the cashews not too fine or cut them with a knife into small pieces.

3 In a container, mix all the ingredients and let it sit for a minimum of 2 hours (until the coconut has macerated well).

4 With a mold, make small squares with the prepared dough.

5 Refrigerate for about 2 hours and remove the mold.

Note: It can be served in this way, but also it lasts a while if it is dehydrated until you have the desired texture.

Its flavor, shape, and smell reach the core.

I am radiant

Peach ice cream

6⅔ cups (1 kg) peach • ⅔ cups (100 g) cashews • 1 banana • 4 teaspoons (20 ml) lemon juice

1. Peel the peaches and remove the pits. Also peel the banana.

2. Place the peaches, banana, cashews, and lemon juice in the blender vessel, and blend them until you've made a homogenous cream.

3. Distribute the cream in individual containers and keep them in the freezer.

Summer, heat . . . Refresh yourself with this delicious ice cream.

I am surprising

Beet and apple cookies

4 cups (500 g) apples • ⅔ cup (90 g) beets • ⅓ cup (50 g) of cashews • 2 teaspoons (3 g) fresh ginger • 1 spoonful grated dry coconut

1. Soak the cashews for 6 hours. Drain and dehydrate them until they are dry enough. After, grind them into flour.

2. Peel 1¾ cups (300 g) of apples and beets. Blend these two ingredients with the ginger.

3. Peel and grate 1¼ cups (200 g) of apples and mix them with the cashew flour, the grated dry coconut, and the pulp from the blending of the apple, beet, and ginger juice, until you've made a dough.

4. Shape cookies from the dough and place them on a dehydrator tray, on a sheet of teflex. Dehydrate for 12 hours.

5. Take out the teflex sheet, turn over the cookies, and dehydrate for 3 hours more or until you've reached the desired texture.

Note: These cookies are conceived by being able to enjoy the excess pulp from the resulting juice of the apples, beets, and ginger (see recipe **I am thoroughbred**, p. 206).

I am generosity
Hazelnut cookies

1⅓ cups (200 g) hazelnut • ½ cup (80 g) apple • ½ teaspoon (2.5ml) cinnamon tea • 4 teaspoons (20 ml) lemon juice • 6 tablespoons (80 ml) agave • a pinch of salt

1 Soak the hazelnut for 24 hours. Once this time has passed, drain well.

2 Blend them in the food processor until you have a fine texture, as if you were trying to make a moist flour.

3 Next, add the cinammon, agave, and lemon juice to it. Mix again and pour the mixture in a bowl.

4 Peel the apple, grate it very finely, and add it to the mixture. Stir carefully with a wooden spoon.

5 Place the preparation on a dehydrator tray, atop a teflex sheet. Spread it out, and, with the help of a mold, cut it in the shape of cookies.

6 Dehydrate for 6 hours.

7 Once this time has passed, turn them over and dehydrate for 3 more hours.

8 These hazelnut cookies can also be eaten without dehydrating them. In this case, keep them in the refrigerator.

Note: If you want to conserve them for some time, you will have to dehydrate them until they are very dry.

Crunchy, sweet, and ideal for a winter afternoon.

I am gratitude

Cashew and coconut cookies

1⅖ cups (200 g) cashews • 1 cup (90 g) coconut powder • 7½ tablespoons (100 ml) agave

1 Soak the cashews for 6 hours, drain them, and dehydrate until they are very dry.

2 Next, grind them until you have made powder.

3 Mix the cashew and coconut powders and add the agave, little by little, until you have a dense dough to make cookies.

4 Mold it in the shape that you want and dehydrate until they are dry.

Note: These cookies last for a few days when completely dehydrated.

One cookie, two, three . . . they will release your passion.

I am generosity

I am surprising

I am gratitude

Juices, Shakes, and Other Drinks

In just a few minutes we can prepare healthy, nutritious, and delicious juices, shakes, and other drinks with a variety of flavors, textures, aromas, and colors.

I am aroma

Cucumber, celery, and fennel juice

4 cups (430 g) cucumber • 4 tablespoons (15 g) ginger • 1⅕ cups (120 g) celery • 4 tablespoons (60 ml) lemon juice • 1 cup (90 g) fennel

1 Peel the cucumbers.

2 Wash the celery and fennel.

3 Put the cucumber, ginger, celery and fennel in the blender.

4 Upon serving, add the lemon juice.

A refreshing, lightly acidic juice.

I am wild

Carrot juice

3⅔ cups (460 g) apples • ⅔ cup (55 g) cabbage leaves • 2 cups (280 g) carrots • ⅗ cup (60 g) celery stalk • less than one lime (10 g) with the peel • 2 teaspoons (3 g) ginger

1 Peel and cut the apples and carrots.

2 Wash the cabbage leaves, celery, and lime.

3 Blend all the ingredients and serve immediately.

I am honesty

Pineapple and spinach juice

1¼ cup (200 g) pineapple without rind or core • 1 cup (100 g) of cucumber • 2 cups (60 g) spinach • 3–4 teaspoons (7 g) ginger • ½ lemon (8 g) with peel

1 Peel and cut the cucumber.

2 Wash the spinach.

3 Next, blend all the ingredients. Serve immediately.

A delicious juice to enjoy on a hot summer night.

Pineapple

It is a tropical fruit that, if it has matured well, has a sweet flavor (if it hasn't matured well, it is more acidic). To know the level of maturation, it is suggested to feel it to verify that it yields, a little, to the pressure of your fingers. Another way is checking the ease with which its central leaves come off. It provides carbohydrates, a little protein, and barely any fat. It is also rich in potassium, magnesium, folates, vitamin C, and, in a smaller portion, vitamins B1 (thiamine) and B6 (pyridoxine). But, above all its components, the strong action of an enzyme (bromelain) that helps to digest proteins stands out the most. The consumption of pineapple is, in addition, an antioxidant, laxative, and diuretic.

I am thoroughbred

Apple and beet juice with a touch of lemon and ginger

2⅖ cups (300 g) apples • ⁷⁄₁₀ cup (90 g) of beet • 1 teaspoon (3 g) fresh ginger • a few drops of lemon juice

1 Peel the apples and beet.

2 Blend all the ingredients.

3 Add a few drops of lemon juice.

Optional: The pulp that is left over from the blending can be used to make some cookies (see recipe *I am surprising*, p. 198).

A juice that will surprise us and with which we will feel full of vitality.

I am refreshing

Strawberry shake with ice cream

2 cups (290 g) strawberries • 1⅖ cups (200 g) ice cream • ⅘ cup (200 ml) of water • 6 tablespoons (80 ml) agave • ¼ cup (32 g) macadamia nuts (optional)

1 Wash the strawberries and remove the leaves.

2 Place all the ingredients in the blender vessel and blend well.

* * * *

Note: With the macadamia nuts, the shake is creamier.

It is a very fresh, delicious shake.

I am a feather

Almond milk

Light, soft . . .we will feel like we're on a cloud.

2 cups (300 g) raw almonds with the shell • 5 tablespoons (70 ml) agave • 4 cups (1 l) water

1 Soak the almonds for 48 hours; change the water every 12 hours.

2 Drain, wash, and peel the almonds.

3 Place them in the blender vessel together with the water and blend.

4 Arrange a colander on top of a bowl and, atop it, spread a cotton cloth. Pour the almond liquid and strain. To extract all of the milk, close up the bowl with the cloth and, with your hands, apply as much pressure as you can.

5 Place the milk in the blender once again, add the agave, and beat.

I am perfection

Sesame seed milk

⅘ cup (120 g) of sesame seeds • 3 tablespoons (40 ml) agave • 4 cups (1 l) water

1 Wash the sesame seeds and soak them for 6 hours. After, drain them.

2 Place them, with the water, in the blender vessel and blend.

3 Arrange a colander on top of a bowl, and, above the bowl, spread a cotton cloth. Pour the liquid in and strain. To extract all of the milk, close up the bowl with the cloth and, with your hands, put pressure on as much of it that you can.

4 Place the milk in the blender vessel, add the agave, and mix it all well.

Note: To sweeten the milk, instead of agave, you can use some dates. In this case, to make the milk, you have to blend the sesame seeds with the dates and water. Next, strain the resulting liquid according to the aforementioned procedure.

The excess pulp from the sesame seed milk is not usually used because it is very bitter.

Vegetable milks

Vegetable milks, such as those prepared with sesame seeds, almonds, pine nuts, or hazelnuts, provide quality nutrients, including proteins with vegetable origins and unsaturated fats. They are made with water and, sometimes, a natural sweetener like agave, dates, or honey, which are very healthy.

I am awakening

Hazelnut milk with cocoa

1½ cups (200 g) of hazelnut • ½ cup (140 ml) agave • 4 tablespoons (20 g) cocoa • 4 cups (1 l) water

1 Soak the hazelnuts for about 24 hours. After, drain and wash them.

2 Place the hazelnuts and water in the blender vessel and blend.

3 Arrange a colander on top of a bowl, and above it, spread out a cotton cloth. Pour the liquid in and strain. To extract all the milk, close up with the cloth and, with your hands, put as much pressure on it as you can.

4 Next, place the milk in the blender vessel and add the cocoa and agave. Mix all of it well, and, before serving, let it chill in the refrigerator for 1 hour.

❋ ❋ ❋ ❋

Note: The excess pulp from straining the milk can be dehydrated (atop a teflex sheet) until it is dried well. Afterward, keep it inside a tightly sealed jar, in a place that is dry and fresh, so you can use it when you want. It doesn't have a taste and is served as an ingredient in soups, sweets, shakes . . .

A consistent milk to refresh yourself in the summer and to savor in the winter.

I am a feather

I am awakening

I am perfection

I am adventure

Apple and tomato juice

2½ cups (310 g) apples • 1 cup (175 g) tomato • 1¼ cups (210 g) pineapple without the skin or core • 3 teaspoons (6 g) ginger • salt • pepper

1 Wash and cut up the apples and tomatoes.

2 Afterward, blend them together with the rest of the ingredients, except the salt and pepper, which will be added upon serving.

A perfect combination of ingredients for a gourmet appetizer.

I am air

Cucumber and apple juice

2⅔ cups (330 g) apples • ⅞ cup (90 g) of cucumber • ⅔ cup (70 g) of celery • ½ small lemon (7 g) with peel • 1 tablespoon (4 g) parsley

1 Wash and cut up the cucumber and apples.

2 Wash the celery and lemon.

3 Blend all the ingredients and serve immediately.

Discover a delicious flavor between sweet and bitter.

I am speed

Orange and pineapple shake with greens

2¾ cups (470 g) orange • 2 cups (350 g) pineapple • 1 tablespoon (4 g) parsley • ⅓ cup (35 g) celery • 4 tablespoons (10 g) radish greens • ⅔ cup (50 g) endive leaves • ½ cup (100 ml) water

1 Peel the orange to the edge.

2 Peel the pineapple and take out the core.

3 Wash the parsley, celery, radish leaves, and endive leaves.

4 Place all in the blender vessel and blend until you have a fine shake.

A smooth chlorophyll shake.

I am exceptional

Pear, pineapple, celery, and spinach shake

3 cups (500 g) pineapple • 1 cup (250 g) pear • ½ cup (45 g) celery • 2 cups (60 g) fresh spinach • 7 tablespoons (105 ml) water

1 Wash the spinach and celery.

2 Peel the pineapple and remove the core.

3 Peel the pear and remove the seeds.

4 Place all the ingredients in the blender vessel and blend until you have a fine texture.

A spectacular mix.

I am regenerative

Rejuvelac

⅗ cup (100 g) soft wheat • 4 cups (1 l) of water for each phase rejuvelac

1 Soak the seeds for 8–10 hours.

2 Drain, rinse, and let the seeds germinate for a couple of days (following the process of germinating seeds in the usual way).

3 Once germinated, add water, surpassing the volume of the seeds two times, and let it sit at room temperature for 48 hours with a mosquito net atop the opening of the glass jar.

4 Once this time has passed, we have rejuvelac. Remove the liquid from the jar without taking off the mosquito net and keep the jar in the refrigerator.

5 You can make another rejuvelac with the same germinated seeds. Put in the same amount of water and let it sit for 24 hours. Then, strain, and now we can use it. Keep refrigerated.

6 Once again, it can be made into rejuvelac. The same process is repeated, and, once strained, we can throw away the seeds.

Note: The taste is influenced by the type of seeds, the times that they have been washed, the water used, the place where it ferments . . . It is a live food and, thus, its changes are constant. Usually, the first rejuvelac is lighter than the second, and the second is lighter than the third. A well-made rejuvelac is a muddy liquid that is a light yellowish with an acidic, true yeast-like flavor. When the process is quickened and not enough time is allowed, it can make a weak, lightly bitter rejuvelac, and if extra time is allowed, it can have a taste that is bitter or sweet, that although it is not damaging, it can be discarded. At times, it can be a little carbonated as a result of fermentation. It is conserved a maximum of 3–4 days in the fridge. Rejuvelac can also be made from quinoa, millet, spelt, and kamut grains.

I am extraordinary

Wheatgrass juice

Blades of wheatgrass

I   Put the green blades in the manual or electric blender (electric is preferred for wheat grass).

A bunch of blades ⅘ inches (2 cm) thick should be sufficient, for each round. The pulp can be pressed to extract the most juice possible.

✳   ✳   ✳   ✳

Note: If you have never had this juice before, it is better to start with very small amounts. For example, try 1 or 2 soupspoons-worth and gradually have more until you get to an amount that feels right. Generally, between ⅛ and ½ cup (30 and 120 ml) is sufficient. To maximize its properties, it's better to drink it fast, 10 minutes after having had a glass of water. It is recommended to consume slowly, and not to eat anything until it has been digested (30–45 minutes). Its taste is slightly sweet and pleasant, although there are people who don't like it, so it is possible to add it to other vegetable or fruit juices. It is a great natural detoxifying food, which helps to regenerate and protect the organism, in addition to being a good antioxidant and preventing cellular aging.

Chlorophyll
Chlorophyll, considered the "blood" of the plants, and sunlight are fundamental to the creation of organic material. This material has a chemical structure that is very similar to the structure of hemoglobin: the only difference is that chlorophyll possesses a magnesium atom, while hemoglobin possesses an iron atom.

I am vital

Solar water with aromas

Water • fruit and/or aromatic herbs to your liking • stevia in a liquid of your liking

1 Pour the water into a glass jar, together with aromatic herbs or fruit of your liking (for example, strawberries, lemon . . .).

2 Let the jar be exposed to the sun for 1 day, from the morning to the evening.

3 Finally, drain the water and add the amount of stevia that you want.

Enjoy this infusion full of energy. It is your best energizing drink.

I am infinite

Fresh water

1 cup (250 ml) of orange juice • 4 cups (1 l) of natural water • ¼ cup (75 ml) of agave

1 Mix all the ingredients and refrigerate.

Note: This delicious refreshment can be made with other fruit juices: melon, strawberry, watermelon . . . You just have to substitute the orange juice for the juice of your choice and adjust the amount of agave to the taste of each one. If sparkling water is used, it is also very delicious.

Water

It is the indispensable element to maintain hydration. It doesn't have calories and it satisfies the thirst for many hours.

I am illumination

Fig and hibiscus flower infusion

1 cup (160 g) dry figs • ⅛ cup (5 g) dry hibiscus flowers • 1 teaspoon (2 g) dry stevia leaves • 4 cups (1 l) water

1 In a bowl, prepare the water with the figs, hibiscus flowers, and stevia.

2 Let it rest for a minimum of 12 hours.

3 Strain the liquid and the infusion, so it is ready to serve.

Note: It can also be marinated with a bit of lime or lemon peel.

Surprising.

Hibiscus flower

Its components provide many virtues. Amongst them are its effects on the digestive system and intestinal regulation, as well its effects on hypertension, varicose veins, atherosclerosis, and, above all, its soothing quality, which helps soothe the mucus membranes of the respiratory channels.

I am illumination

I am vital

I am infinity

Index of Recipes

JUICES, SHAKES, AND OTHER DRINKS